Out of Place

An Autoethnography of Postcolonial Citizenship

Nuraan Davids

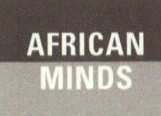

Published in 2022 by African Minds
4 Eccleston Place, Somerset West, 7130, Cape Town, South Africa
info@africanminds.org.za | www.africanminds.org.za

© 2022 African Minds

All contents of this document, unless specified otherwise, are licensed under a
Creative Commons Attribution 4.0 International License.

The views expressed in this publication are those of the author.
When quoting from any of the chapters, readers are requested to acknowledge the author.

ISBN (paper): 978-1-928502-36-4
eBook edition: 978-1-928502-37-1
ePub edition: 978-1-928502-38-8

Copies of this book are available for free download at: www.africanminds.org.za

ORDERS:
African Minds
Email: info@africanminds.org.za

To order printed books from outside Africa, please contact:
African Books Collective
PO Box 721, Oxford OX1 9EN, UK
Email: orders@africanbookscollective.com

Contents

Foreword by Jonathan D Jansen v
Acknowledgements ix
Frequently used abbreviations and acronyms x

Chapter 1: And so, I choose to (re)write 1

Chapter 2: Autoethnography: A counter-narrative of experiences 13

Chapter 3: Race as disqualifying disfigurement 31

Chapter 4: Parents (not) for Change 55

Chapter 5: Lost in diversity 77

Chapter 6: (Dis)embodied intersectionality 95

Chapter 7: Patriarchy as religion 111

Chapter 8: Postscript: Through the doorway 131

References 135
Index 149
About the author 159

Foreword

This is the most powerful academic biography you will ever read on the politics of place in South Africa as revealed through the story of a human life. The book gives away the plot in its opening sentence, at once eloquent and devastating: 'Long before I first realised it, I had learnt to take careful note of where I was before I could decide how to be.' It is this particular pillar of learning once articulated by Jacques Deloris (learning to know, learning to do, learning to live together – with others) that the author, Nuraan Davids, teaches through a gripping and disturbing set of personal stories.

If there is a research question that guides the telling, it is this: How do you learn to be as a 'coloured', hijab-wearing Muslim woman in a country that itself is still struggling with how to be towards its own citizens, let alone those from other African countries? Like all people of conscience, the very designation 'coloured' is used on an exceptional basis, to make a point, for what Mzansi does is place you inside identity boxes that once thrilled the apartheid masters. That is the point: How to be in relation to this lingering placeholder that continues to carry so much currency including among those happy to be referred to as 'mixed race' – distinct from the presumably pure races, the 'African' and 'Indian' and, the purest of them all, the 'whites'.

Not all Muslim women wear the hijab, a blessing to the devout, a marker that singles you out in a crowd for this is not the place, post-apartheid South Africa with its glorious constitution, for how to be a good Muslim. That founding document was supposed to guarantee a place in the sun for every citizen regardless of colour or creed; a document cannot do that, of course, its all-inclusive language notwithstanding.

It is as if being a woman in a country with one of the highest rates of violence towards women was not enough. The words are even bandied around in die volksmond (literally, in the everyday spoken language of ordinary people) as if its traumatic meaning speaks for itself: gender-based violence. Every newsreader and every public official repeat the term until it loses all meaning even as the assault on women's bodies continues: GBV, is the printed abbreviation.

Learning how to be as a woman in education and society is a vital thread that runs through the book, one that is knotted together with those other intersectional threads: 'coloured', hijab-wearing, Muslim woman.

Unsurprisingly, the book opens with the politics of dis-placement. Where not to be, in other words. In Cape Town, the setting for the book, this is one of those unspeakable traumas – the mass displacement of 'coloured' people from their homes in order to make place for 'whites'. The author learns quickly that this is not her place even if generations of family members might have lived in the house and in the area. But this forced dislodging from your home is not only about physical displacement. It is also about the disconnection, nay disruption, of relationships that were once acceptable between 'black' and 'white' children and their families.

It is in telling the story of being out-of-place as far as home is concerned that the author's emotional detachment from place is most sharply articulated. Uprooted from your birthplace sounds and feels more accurate. You do not belong here was the message then, and now.

One of 'the firsts' to enter 'white' schools in the early years of desegregation, as a student teacher and then later as a qualified educator, the author walks right into it all over again. She would experience something that scholars are only starting to talk about almost three decades since the end of legal apartheid: racial resentment against these early interlopers in lily-white schools as learners, then teachers and more recently, principals. The author stands out as a hijab-wearing Muslim woman of colour and learns very quickly that for all those reasons she is once more out of place. Curiously, the learners accept her; the teachers and her seniors struggle with how to be with her, and with the new country. For months, the old and the new South African flags fly alongside each other in the school where she teaches.

By the time the author leaves school teaching for university, one would expect a more tolerant environment where academic citizens are usually admired for standing out and, as higher education mythology has it, paid to think for themselves. Not so, for in this conservative, Afrikaans, patriarchal university with its roots in Dutch Calvinism, you are out place long before you set foot on campus.

But the hard lines of institutional exclusion have long softened, if not disappeared and so the author is able to rise to professorial status within her university and even become a head of department in education policy studies. However, another place-based struggle then emerges when she applies for the deanship and loses out to a 'black' African man. She enjoys majority support of the faculty and the senate whose votes are discarded by the council and the 'black' man appointed.

Given that the Western Cape has a long and tragic history of exclusion of Africans whom, in the apartheid imaginary, belonged elsewhere in one of the 'black' homelands (Bantustans), this is clearly a welcome appointment. But the author asks us to take a closer look. She too is 'black', in the broader sense of the inclusive term held by progressives. She is a woman in an institution that has never had a female academic leader at the top. She is a Muslim woman, a hijab-wearing one, in a place that started off 100 years ago with a faculty of Christian theology.

What she feels is yet another out-of-place experience even if this time the appointment of a 'black' male dean is a good thing for her university. In other words, this is one instance upon many others where the accumulated experience of being out-of-place cuts deep.

Off-campus is no different. The author learns quickly that place is unstable and treacherous at the same time. A security guard in a shopping centre with whom she is on nodding terms becomes the instrument for corporate Islamophobia on the day after 9/11. A Muslim woman's bags must be searched presumably for explosive devices. The airport of course is a familiar place for Islamic surveillance. The humiliation never stops, the sense of being out-of-place continues.

All institutions are implicated in ensuring that a 'coloured', hijab-wearing, Muslim woman is kept in her place. The only thing worse than school or university is a woman having a critical voice, raising troubling questions and pushing back against rigid traditions within her own religious community. Nothing hurts more than being seen and indeed treated as out-of-place in your faith community.

How does one learn to be in such treacherous times and in so many troubled places? This is what the author Nuraan Davids teaches without being didactic, and shows without being pedantic. Place has to be constantly negotiated and fought for. It has to be coloured in with new meanings, even transformed. Place is inevitably political, open to some and closed-off to others.

In sharing her painful navigations crossing difficult terrain, the author does something really momentous in this book: she teaches us how to be in troubled spaces and, in the process, makes democratic places more open, more hospitable and more inclusive for generations to come. For that reason alone, this book should be required reading.

Jonathan D Jansen
Stellenbosch University
February 2022

Acknowledgements

Deep gratitude is due to the following:

- Stellenbosch University for granting me a research opportunity which allowed me the time to focus exclusively on my writing.
- My fellowship at the Center for Advanced Study in the Behavioral Sciences (CASBS) at Stanford University (2020–2021). The privilege of this experience provided me with the head- and heart-space to reflect not only upon my work, but on who I am as an academic.
- I am especially grateful to Allison Stanger who offered invaluable comments on initial chapter drafts.
- Aaliyah, for the book cover idea.
- Jonathan Jansen, for graciously writing the foreword to this book.
- My colleagues, for their encouragement and critique.

Frequently used abbreviations and acronyms

ACSA	Airports Company South Africa
ANC	African National Congress
CCMA	Commission for Conciliation, Mediation and Arbitration
CNE	Christian National Education
DA	Democratic Alliance
DP	Democratic Party
DHET	Department of Higher Education and Training
DoE	Department of Education
ECD	Early Childhood Development
FA	Federal Alliance
HoE	Head of Education
HDE	Higher Diploma in Education
HR	Human Resources
HRC	Human Rights Commission (South Africa)
IP	Independent Party
INPE	International Network of Philosophers Education
MSA	Muslim Students Association
MYM	Muslim Youth Movement
NDM	National Democratic Movement
NNP	New National Party

FREQUENTLY USED ABBREVIATIONS AND ACRONYMS

OBE	Outcomes-Based Education
PGCE	Postgraduate Certificate in Education
PBUH	Peace Be Upon Him
PfC	Parents for Change
PFP	Progressive Federal Party
SGB	School Governing Body
SMT	School Management Team
UCT	University of Cape Town
USAf	Universities South Africa
UWC	University of the Western Cape
WCED	Western Cape Education Department

For Thabiet

Raise your words, not voice.
It is rain that grows flowers,
not thunder.
– Rumi

1

And so, I choose to (re)write

Long before I first realised it, I had learnt to take careful note of where I was before I could decide how to be. Neither the realisation, nor the unconscious action of observing before acting, is especially strange – at least, not if you have spent most of your life watching and waiting in the way I have. Admittedly, the hardest part of this realisation is that the more I have attempted to make sense of myself in relation to the worlds in which I live and visit, the deeper my sense of struggle and conflict. I vacillate, quite vividly, at times, between memories of childhood friendships and adult disappointments. There was Anna-Marie, for instance, with whom I shared daily walks from school. I know there were whisperings of them moving – I think her mother might have mentioned it to me one late afternoon as I was about to head home. But, for some reason, I still cannot remember when exactly Anna-Marie and her family left. I can only recall knocking on their front door a few times before realising that not only was nobody home, but the house was empty. Their departure seemed to set into motion a ripple effect of removal trucks and removed friendships – normally on a Saturday, with neighbours lifting furniture, amid hugs of promising to stay in touch.

A silence settled in our street. And I began to befriend the new girl next door, Marion. She did not attend the same school as me. Hers was much nicer. I remember recognising it through the back window of my father's car as I caught sight of girls wearing the same uniform as Marion. I don't think Marion and I liked each other very much. We were the only two girls in our street. I think the boredom forced us into each other's company. We were awkward in our girlhood chatter. I remember her father was 'white', but her mother was 'coloured'. I mention this only because it was an odd union to witness at the time. A time of which I had little understanding, even as I lived and experienced it. I don't know what happened to Marion. The next removal truck came for my family.

It would be a year later that I would first begin to assign names and understandings to South Africa's apartheid, its residential segregation and forced removals, its racism, its hatred, its fractures. High school saw me initiated into a politics of resistance, of protests and rallies in the place of abandoned lessons. It was a time of invigorated hope – mostly convinced by our untested youth. It was also a time of deep despair and fear – deepened by our individual inability to formulate. As a collective, it all made sense – the rallying calls and demands for change, the release of Nelson Mandela, for a freedom which we could only understand in relation to that which we had not yet experienced. Schoolmates would disappear overnight; someone would reappear, others never did. We lived and experienced a time few of us could truly understand. And maybe it was best that we could not fully comprehend the sheer depravity and obscenity of apartheid. After all, how does one process such immorality through a consciousness of innocence? There are reasons that we keep certain images, words, actions and violence from children. Theirs is a vulnerability that once tainted cannot be restored. Such are the lives of those blotted by apartheid – a dehumanisation enforced by those who cannot but be dehumanised themselves. It reminds me of Das's (2007: 4) observation that 'we learn about the nature of the world in the process of such living'.

The idea for this book, even as I write these sentences, has still not been fully thought through. What was meant to be an exploratory analysis of alterity – specifically, what it means to be seen and perceived as 'other' – slowly slid into struggles which I thought I had laid to rest through previous writings. Maybe it is the timing of the writing – the restrictions imposed by an altered world, dictated by a global pandemic, or the fact that I am on research leave from my university allowing me an indulgence of time I have never appreciated enough. Or maybe it was the fact that I had read George Orwell's (1946) essay, 'Why I write' for a second time. I first read it as a naïve undergraduate student, probably at the same time when I read Roland Barthes' 'Death of the author'.

Orwell (1946) explains that a writer's 'subject-matter will be determined by the age he lives in ... but before he ever begins to write he will have acquired an emotional attitude from which he will never completely escape'. He famously identified that writers, to varying degrees, and depending on their contexts, are driven by four motives to write. One is sheer egoism – a 'desire to seem clever, to be talked about, to be remembered after death, to get your own back on grown-ups who snubbed you in childhood ... But there is also the minority of gifted, wilful people who are determined to live their own lives to the end, and writers belong in this class.' Second is aesthetic enthusiasm – a 'perception of beauty in the external world, or, on the other hand, in words and their right arrangement'. Third is historical impulse – a 'desire to see things as they are, to find out true facts and store them up for the use of posterity'. And fourth is political purpose – a 'desire to push the world in a certain direction, to alter other people's idea of the kind of society that they should strive after' (Orwell, 1946).

I see myself and my writing reflected in all of Orwell's possibilities. While my ability to assign emotional cognition to it arose later in my life, I intuitively knew that my attitude towards the world was disfigured by a knowledge that I somehow fell short of whatever criteria had been set as acceptable. My own disfigured impression of the world has been somewhat subdued by age and time, especially while living in surroundings of significant political reform, but the world, unfortunately, has not become any less of a disfiguring place. I come to my writing with an intention of re-figuring myself. The unequivocal claim of this writing as my own renders it free from the grip of those who repeatedly claim to know my story, who, in their efforts to speak and write on my behalf, over me, down to me, succeed only in erasing any trace of who I truly am. The self-proclaimed beauty of this writing is so for no other reason but that it is written by someone who, had I believed my apartheid masters, should never have been able to write in the first place.

My purpose, therefore, first, is to push myself into a world in which women who look like me, are de facto cast as oppressed and voiceless. There are pre-judgements, if not about the colour of my skin, then my gender, and if not either of these two, then both, or my religion, and of late, if not my religion, then my hijab. Each marker adds another dimension, another (dis)embodiment – until I am no longer just human, but an intersectional appellation of race, ethnicity, culture, gender and religion.

Each embodiment is accompanied by the weight of its own connotations. These connotations are imposed from the outside, they dissect and disfigure me into *what I am* (mis)perceived to be, rather than *who I am*. They come from without, they are imposed, which has seldom not served as disfigurement. My writing, though fraught in its depictions and experiences of marginalisation, exclusion and oppression, is a means of undoing the disfigurement, of freeing myself from the biases and myths of what my identities seemingly provoke.

My second purpose is, I write not *for* you, but *to* you. I write to you as an acknowledged agreement with Barthes (1977: 5–6), that a text 'consists of multiple writings, issuing from several cultures and entering into dialogue with each other, into parody, into contestation; but there is one place where this multiplicity is collected, united, and this place is not the author, as we have hitherto said it was, but the reader'. While the writing is mine, the text is yours. In Sparkes' (2007: 540) words, 'I have chosen to offer a story for consideration, then the story must do its work, on its own, as a story.' I neither can, nor want, to control how my writing is interpreted from different and unique perspectives. Like Sparkes (2007: 540), my only 'hope is that the reader might think *with* the story and see where it takes them.' Some readers might find resonance and familiarity, others might remain unmoved, even sceptical.

For me, this book takes me on a retrospective journey – one which signals my tiredness with being framed by theoretical debates and arguments, which are about me, but fail to see or recognise me. But perhaps, more than that, it is what Saidiya Hartman (2008) describes as a sense longing, which arises from loss. Something un-happens when a life is en-framed, dictated, restricted and reduced. There are yearnings for what could have been, should have been. The constant side-lining, overlooking and exclusion write themselves onto who I am and who I become, creating a scepticism in the world around me.

A postcolonial autoethnography

My life has been marked by experiences which I recognise as shared with others but not the same as others'. There are exacting experiences and knowledge which imprint on us – as an oppressed collective, as women, as women of colour, as Muslim women, as hijab-wearing Muslim women, experiences which would be unknown to an individual who embodies none of these descriptors. Das (2007: 41) captures this sense as follows:

> My knowledge of you marks me, it is something that I experience, yet I am not present to it ... My knowledge of myself is something I find, as on a successful quest, my

> knowledge of others, of their separateness from me, is something that finds me ... And it seems reasonable to me, and illuminating, to speak of that reception of impression as my lending my body to the other's experience.

While I am attuned to the knowledge, and live with the impressions of others, I cannot make sense of their stories without taking account of mine first. I know of their lives and their stories through my own witnessing. I can imagine myself in their emotions when they suffer at the words and actions of discrimination and 'othering', I can retell their stories only to the extent of what I know, but I cannot recapture their stories without losing the essence of their pain, loss and displacement. I can imagine what it might be like for a refugee to flee her home by foot, with no more than a single bag, containing her life's value. I can imagine her dread, her hopelessness, but I cannot lay claim to knowing her true trauma without being her. I cannot speak on her behalf any more or less than I can speak on behalf of all women, or Muslim women, or any semblance of a community for that matter. To do so would not only imply a undifferentiated understanding of communities, but that communities are undifferentiated in the first place. Moreover, to do so would be to fall into a misleading rhetoric of colonisation which prides itself on a misrepresentation of *all* women and, in particular, women who are not 'white', as not only a fixed category but fixed as victims (Mohanty, 1988; Radcliffe, 1994).

I am of the view that it is not enough to consider only what we know, it is equally necessary to interrogate how we have come to know what we know. This view might be implicit within conceptions of epistemology – as more than just a way of knowing, but also systems and processes of knowing that are linked to worldviews based on the conditions under which people live and learn (Ladson-Billings, 2000). The problem, however, remains a predominance of Anglo-normative epistemologies which often overshadow or, worse, misrepresent or erase, other forms of knowledge production. In response, explains Young (2009), postcolonial theory has been created from the political insights and experience that were developed during colonial resistance to Western rule and cultural dominance, primarily during the course of the anti-colonial struggles of the 19th and 20th centuries. Instead of theoretical rigidity and dogmatism, maintains Young (2009: 14), postcolonial theory contains 'a spirit of innovation and a desire to combine universal ideas of social justice with the realities of local cultures and their particular conditions.'

Starting with the deconstruction of ethnocentric assumptions in Western knowledge, postcolonial studies mark the intrusion of radically different perspectives into the academy (Young, 2009), as well as knowledge. Importantly, while the prefix 'post' might infer a period 'after', 'colonialism's economic, political and cultural deformative traces' are in the present (Shohat, 1992: 105). For the most part, explains Maldonado-Torres (2016: 10), colonialism and decolonisation are usually depicted as 'historical episodes ... locked in the past, located elsewhere, or confined to specific empirical dimensions'. Generally, colonialism is used to refer to the strategy of European political domination from the 16th to the 20th centuries.

Yet, contrary to being 'locked in the past', colonialism is neither restricted to a specific time nor a particular place. In other words, just because colonialism is a part of a particular society's history does not mean that the impact of colonialism is no longer evident or felt. Instead of eroding, colonialism morphs and adopts different forms within different contexts. It is the residual influence of colonisation, its messiness and contradictions (Sium et al. 2012), which brings into contestation notions of decolonisation. It is this messiness which prompts me to rely on a postcolonialism as a 'constant interrogation', 'a possibility that is "not yet" but that may announce the prospect of "something new"' (De Oliveira et al., 2012: 2).

Postcolonialism, explains Young (2003: 3), offers you a way of seeing things differently, 'a language and a politics in which you come first, not last'. Western knowledge relies on binary oppositions: instead of master–slave, man–woman, civilised–uncivilised, culture–barbarism, modern–primitive, coloniser–colonised. In seeking to undo the demonising effect of these binary constructions, postcolonialism seeks to develop a different paradigm in which identities are no longer starkly oppositional or exclusively singular but defined by their intricate and mutual relations with others (Young, 2009). Postcolonialism, therefore, begins from its own counter-knowledges and from the diversity of its cultural experiences. It offers a language of and for those who have no place, who seem not to belong, of those whose knowledges and histories are not allowed to count (Young, 2009). In this vein, a number of scholars have begun talking about critical raced and raced-gendered epistemologies that emerge from the social, cultural and political (Bernal, 2000). Bernal (2002: 107) explains that these 'raced and raced-gendered epistemologies directly challenge the broad range of currently popular research paradigms, from positivism to constructivism and liberal feminism to postmodernism, which draw from a narrow foundation of knowledge that is based on the social, historical and cultural experiences of Anglos'.

One notable example is that of Hartman, who has done compelling work by conceptualising and using 'critical fabulation', as a mode of storytelling that involves subjunctive and critical speculation on the gaps and silences of official archival records relating to the transatlantic slave-trade. The intention here, explains Hartman (2008: 11), 'isn't anything as miraculous as recovering the lives of the enslaved or redeeming the dead, but rather laboring to paint as full a picture of the lives of the captives as possible'. She describes her method as 'straining against the limits of the archive to write a cultural history of the captive and, at the same time, enacting the impossibility of representing the lives of the captives precisely through the process of narration' (Hartman, 2008: 11). Hartman (2008: 11) considers stories 'as a form of compensation or even as reparations, perhaps the only kind we will ever receive'.

This writing is my story, my autoethnography – my reparation, if you will. I am not distant from it; I stand right in the centre of it, with the purpose of forwarding a perspective, which not only contributes, shares and fills certain gaps, but brings into question the establishment of certain dominant narratives. Like Hartman (2008), I think of stories as restorative, not only in the sense of filling in the missing pieces or words, but in terms of restoring dignity and justice. When I tell my story, I am gathering 'knowledge *from* the past and not necessarily knowledge *about* the past' (Bochner, 2007: 203). Narratives, as Farber and Sherry (1995) remind us, de-emphasise conventional analytic measures and instead place more emphasis on the aesthetic and emotional; narratives value 'stories from the bottom' – that is, stories from women, people of colour, people who suffered oppression. The importance and value of narratives reside in an acknowledgement that part of human life and living is talking about it; silence signals oppression (Lugones & Spelman, 1983). Because humans are deeply influenced by what is said about them, they cannot separate their lives from the accounts others have given of them – 'the articulation of our experience is part of our experience' state Lugones and Spelman (1983: 574).

By embarking on an autoethnography, I am not merely trying to change the way my story has been told by others, I am also transforming my 'sense of what it means to live' (Bhabha, 1994: 256). I am driven by a postcolonial appeal which insists that if I wish to imprint my own way of life into the discourses which pervade the world around me then I can no longer allow myself to be spoken on behalf of or to be subjugated into the hegemonies of others. This is not simply about establishing a new narrative. As method and product, autoethnography disrupts the inscribed binary between science and art, between theory and the imagination, and between rationality and emotion (Ellis et al., 2011).

Stories, as Ellis et al. (2011) note, are complex, constitutive, meaningful phenomena that introduce unique ways of thinking and feeling and assist individuals in making sense of themselves and others. Grounded in personal experience, autoethnography holds the potential to 'sensitise readers to issues of identity politics, to experiences shrouded in silence, and to forms of representation that deepen our capacity to empathise with people who are different from us' (Ellis et al., 2011: 274).

Not to tell my story is to infer an untruthful acceptance that things might not be otherwise. The very idea that something might be 'otherwise' is indicative of a particular situatedness, a willingness to provide another perspective – one which sees the world from the bottom up. Insofar as my writing seeks to interrogate the taken-for-granted centres of dominance and subjugation, insofar as I am interested in bringing to the fore and restoring the misappropriated representations of who I am, and ought to be, I situate this writing as a postcolonialist (ad)venture.

In line with Bhabha's (1994) understanding, I do not conceive of postcolonialism as a time *after* colonialism. Rather, a postcolonialism refers to the underlying discourses of colonialism, which have to be interrogated and brought into disrepute. For Bhabha (1994), then, postcolonialism is a theoretical weapon, intent upon resisting certain ideological and political hegemonies. Postcolonialism is as concerned with challenging the insularity of historical narratives and historiographical traditions emanating from Europe, as it is with disrupting dominant assumptive conceptual frameworks which have rendered the 'other' as passive and docile (Bhambra, 2014). My concern and intention echoes that of Bhambra (2014: 116) which is to re-inscribe 'other' cultural traditions into 'narratives of modernity and thus transforming those narratives'. Not only am I embodied by markers of race, ethnicity, culture, gender, sexuality and religion, but my particular set of markers determines how (between hospitality and hostility) I access and participate in certain spaces. I am trapped in a perpetual navigation of sense-making, of explanation, justification, even apology. My 'otherness' enshrouds me, not because of who I am, but because of how I have been marked.

The only way to unsettle both the insularity and distortion of hegemonic narratives is to bring them into contestation through an unmarked knowledge that lives in *who I am*. In bringing into presence who I am, I can potentially make myself known – a politics of 'getting closer' to others 'that will enable the distance and differences between us, to move the political terrain in which it is possible to speak and hear' (Ahmed, 1997: 28–29).

Women's lives, stories and experiences, as feminism seeks to accentuate, have largely been excluded, reduced or invalidated. Although there is widespread consensus that women's experiences must be made visible as an authoritative and unmediated source of knowledge, there are limits and risks to basing politics on essentialist versions of 'women's experience' (Applebaum, 2008). Not only are the social and political categories of my identity (identities) different to that of other women, but the way in which I experience 'othering' and oppression is as distinctive. This recognition places me in a somewhat paradoxical relation(ship) to feminism. I consider it as a methodological lens to centre my experiences as a woman, but I do not trust this lens as a safe and encompassing space of belonging. I am disturbed by a predominance of Western understandings of what constitutes gender exclusion and oppression; I am disturbed by the perpetual casting of 'non-Western' (or third world) women as victims of patriarchy through the vantage point of both 'Western' men and women.

A more accurate description, therefore, would be an employment of critical race feminism as specifically attentive to the marginalisation of women who are not 'white' and, as such, out of the fold of Western feminism. Hence, when I use feminism, I do so with a knowledge that while I am attached and included as a woman, I am excluded and detached as a Muslim woman of colour. Consequently, I see my writing as being grounded in a feminism, directed at subverting systemic and structural hegemonies, including feminism.

In sum, my story is as seeped in the subversion of South Africa's apartheid ideology as it is in being a Muslim woman in a world of increasing Islamophobia. It is wholly possible to frame my narrative as a mere continuation of an anti-apartheid or 'struggle' discourse. It is indeed the case that my experiences as a teacher (discussed in Chapter 2) and as an academic (discussed in Chapter 5) might be ascribed to the residual effects of an apartheid society still trying to find its way to a socially just ethos. The disgraceful deployment of race-based politics during apartheid has yet to leave the shores of democratic South Africa. But I would be hesitant to box my experiences into a particular historical and geopolitical climate. The subjections of scrutiny and 'othering' provoked by my religious identity succeed, at times, in leaving my experiences of racism or sexism in the shadows of my 'othering'. To limit these experiences to a South African context would not only suggest a reduction of the sheer geopolitical span of Islamophobia but would only offer a skewed interpretation of my lived experiences.

My experiences are not limited to a specific locality. The experiences which I have offered in the various chapters of this book are not my totality. They are experiences, distinctive in their influence upon me, but not isolated or singular. They matter insofar as they compel me to self-reflect not only on the specificity of the moment but on the preceding events, contexts, role-players, their meaning for me, and for others, like me, or not like me.

In an oddly ambivalent way, I recognise with relief that I am not alone in my 'othered' trauma and pain. I see my story as a kaleidoscopic reflection of all 'othered' others, whether in the vein of South Africa's struggle politics, America's Black Lives Matter, or 'the state of exception', enforced by an increasing number of European liberal democracies which 'restricts democratic rights under the guise of safeguarding or even expanding them' (Santos, 2007: 16). As a South African the knowledge which I produce is probably more critical now than what it was during apartheid because I am writing this text as a citizen of a democratic state, not an oppressive regime. As a global citizen, my knowledge can serve as a preface to other situated knowledges – unrestricted by borders and unified in its determination to subvert epistemic injustices.

2

Autoethnography:
A counter-narrative of experiences

My experiences matter insofar as they make claims about what lives inside of me, how I move through the world, and the world through me. My experiences matter because they embody who I am, what I know – an embodiment and knowledge, for which I assume responsibility and accountability. There is a certain appeal about the articulation of experiences in that it foregrounds personal voices and vantage points – especially if these vantage points have historically been occupied and shaped by voices and perspectives which have scant ideas of experience as marginalised and subjugated. Let me immediately state, however, that for all the confidence, as well as vulnerability suggested by the writing and sharing of experiences, these experiences are not beyond analysis or interrogation. The idea of speaking on behalf of myself – whether from the sides or below – does not infer an exemption from critique. As Haraway (1988: 583) makes us aware, 'There is a premium on establishing the capacity to see from the peripheries and the depths.' Moreover, she contends, to 'see from below' is neither easily learned nor unproblematic, 'even if "we" "naturally" inhabit the great underground terrain of subjugated knowledges (Haraway, 1988: 584). Critique, therefore, is necessary if I am to enhance and extend my own voice and autonomy. To call something into account as I plan to do by focusing on experiences in this chapter, means that I must take responsibility for these accounts, which, in turn, implies that I have to be willing to subject these accounts to scrutiny. What is it about experiences that assigns them exceptionality? Why is it necessary, if at all, to bring experiences to bear on the theorising of subjugated women, as is my constituted location?

Experiences as lived

To have experience or experiences is to live – to think and feel. Experiences reside and emanate in our perceptions, senses, intuitions, fears, loves, joys, vulnerabilities, disappointments, rejections, successes, failures – our everyday life, thoughts and emotions. Mostly, I am aware of what I experience, there is a certain alertness to what happens around me. I am as conscious of what I say and do (most times), as I am of how others respond to me (or not). Other times, I realise in hindsight that the way in which I understood an experience might not have been the case. Sometimes my annoyance, irritation, or frustration get in the way of what I think I experienced, and that (my experience) only becomes clearer once I am distanced from whatever emotion I felt at the time. I have a general and collective sense, certain stored memories of moments and events, which I consider as defining moments of my life experience. At times, I return to these, I replay them, sometimes with an intention to gain a different perspective, sometimes to think how I might have responded better, smarter, or not at all. Sometimes I consciously go back to a time or place, to rekindle a presence of a lost loved one – as I have repeatedly done with the death of my father over two decades ago. The authority and presence of his life continue to leave an indelible mark on mine.

While some experiences have washed over me – making it hard to discern between reality and blurs of what I think or choose to remember – others keep me in a firm grasp, making it hard to let go, or see beyond particular hurt and mistrust. I have long wondered about the phrase 'have experience'. The phrasing suggests some kind of ownership – as in 'have' – I 'have' experienced how to ride a bicycle, or how to drive a car, so now I 'own' the knowledge of that experience. The phrase is often seen in job advertisements, sometimes more emphatically, as in '*must* have experience' – which, of course, creates immediate barriers for individuals, who might not 'have experience'. In this way, experience is connoted with having knowledge, or skills; experience grants me access to this or that, drawing clear lines between those who are on the inside of the experience, and those who are not. Yet, experience is not limited to what we do or know. It also includes our emotions, sentiments, joys, desires, fears, love and grief. We cannot experience the emotion of loss or despair without experiencing the emotion of love and hope. In the absence of *having* experience, presumably, I neither know what, nor how; I cannot speak of the experience. Presumably, too, I must 'have experience' of experiences to write this particular book. How do I write what I know, and how do I know what to write, without having the experience of either life or writing? Yet, I can, of course, 'have experience' of life without having knowledge of that experience.

At age 13, for example, I experienced being forced to move out of my home. I think the dominant emotion was that of confusion. Even though I had witnessed neighbours leaving and greeting friends as their cars reversed out of driveways, for whatever reason, I was still surprised when it was my family's turn to move. I had so many questions, swirling in my head: where were we moving to? Why couldn't we stay? Would I be reunited with all my friends? Would I have to go to a new school? What if I didn't like it there? Would there be shops near my new home? Would I still be able to play soccer? I knew I did not want to leave that which was known to me. But did I *know* what was happening to me, my family and so many others as South Africa's apartheid eroded lives?

I specifically recall a conversation with my father in which he explained why we had to move. He assured me we would be moving to a 'nice' house, that I would make new friends, and be happy, that he would drive me to school so that I could have the same classmates. The words 'forced removal' or 'apartheid' did not pop up in that conversation. His words cushioned me against the truth of what was really happening. And I believed him. I believed his version of what he chose to tell me – even when it became apparent to me that our new house was certainly not 'nice'. It was smaller than our old home. There were no nearby shops, or soccer fields, or parks, or any of my friends. I felt far away from everything and everybody. Although I never asked him about it, I can only assume protecting me from the vulgarity of apartheid was better than telling me the truth. Were his words 'untruths'? I don't think so. Presumably, his own experiences of 'having' lived through two previous forced removals under the Group Areas Act (No. 41 of 1950) had left him with no choice but to offer me a diluted, less worrying account – to spare me from 'having experience' of being forcefully removed.[1]

The more I write about this 'thing' called experiences, the more I feel it slipping through the lines of these words. Are any of my experiences real? Real in the sense that they have happened as I recall them? Or have I conjured them, shaped them into what *I* felt, what *I* saw, what *I* heard? My subjectivity confirms the potential presence of other 'I's', and hence other vantage points. I cannot be sure, except to hold on to what I know to be my own truth. My truth contains me; I am contained by my truth; my truth is me. Sara Ahmed (2003: 377) says that to make truths is to make 'what is'; it is to bring into

---

1   Passed in 1950, the Group Areas Act imposed control over interracial property transactions and property occupation throughout South Africa; it forced physical separation and segregation between races by creating different residential areas for *each race*. The Group Areas Act displaced hundreds of thousands of people, breaking up families, friends and communities.

existence the 'is' against which the 'truth value' of statements is measured. It is only when this existence or this world becomes 'the given', that decisions can be made about what differentiates true and false statements (Ahmed, 2003: 377). The truth of my experiences, therefore, is not 'the given'; it is, however, *my* given.

When experience is taken as the origin of knowledge, states Scott (1991: 777), the vision of the individual subject 'becomes the bedrock of evidence on which explanation is built'. Questions about the constructed nature of experience, and about how subjects are constituted as different in the first place, are left aside (Scott, 1991). In this way, continues Scott (1991: 777), the evidence of experience 'becomes evidence for the fact of difference, rather than a way of exploring how difference is established, how it operates, how and in what ways it constitutes subjects who see and act in the world'. To her, the evidence of experience reproduces, rather than contests given ideological systems. I concur with Scott's (1991) assertion that when experience is taken as the source of knowledge, the vision of the individual subject becomes the foundation of evidence on which explanation is built. I disagree, however, that this evidence or experience is limited to only a fact of difference, and that it reproduces, rather than questions given ideological systems. Foregrounding experience as difference already begins to pave the ways in which difference is constructed and fostered. The very description and exploration of different experiences subvert the argument not only of normative ideological systems but tilts the idea that all differences are the same by virtue of their differences.

Stated differently, I share a group identity marker with other Muslim women of colour, which might make us different to women of other ideologies. But there are differences within a group of Muslim women, as there are with other group identities, and as there are with the very idea of 'experiences', that not only suggests elusiveness, but destabilises descriptors of homogeneity and fixity. In this sense, following Scott (1991), experience is not the origin of our explanations, but rather that which we seek to explain, that about which knowledge is produced. To think about experience in this way, asserts Scott (1991: 780) 'is to historicise it as well as to historicise the identities it produces'. The appeal of experience is that it is embedded in our daily lives, and hence, embodied in our narratives.

When I share my experiences, I am seeking to provide an account of myself – an intention which confirms an implicit individual and different truth. I am not particularly interested in drawing attention to differences. I trust that readers will do that for themselves – because and regardless of who they are. I am, however, interested in making my story known, for moral, as well as political reasons, and as someone who takes responsibility for myself. As articulated by Lugones and Spelman (1983: 573), 'it matters to us what is said about us, who says it, and to whom it is said: having the opportunity to talk about one's life, to give an account of it, to interpret it, is integral to leading that life rather than being led through it …' To Lugones and Spelman (1983), part of human living and experience is talking about it; to remain silent is to accept the impoverished or degrading descriptions of others – descriptions, which have long ensured the voicelessness of dominated and colonised groups, and in which women especially have experienced pronounced forms of denigration. I am neither alone nor unique in this tension. Such is the predominance of an androcentric worldview, that women's stories or ethnographic intentions, explains Tedlock (2000: 468), are often powered by motives to convince readers of the author's self-worth, 'to clarify and authenticate their self-images'. Hence, the consequent emergence of feminism, which insists upon the presence and enunciation of women's voices and experiences as a counter to the predominance of androcentrism, paternalism and sexism, in theory and in practice.

Autoethnography as a counter-narrative

Storytelling, states Orwell (2017), allows us the uninterrupted space and right to tell others what they do not want to hear. Adopting an autoethnographic approach provides me with the necessary process and product not only to tell my story, but to produce, as described by Geertz (1973: 10), a 'thick description' of my culture in relation to others. By relying on deeply personal reflexive narratives, the autoethnography disrupts conventional understandings of research methodology. In telling and retelling key moments and events, by recalling emotions, I am able to invite insiders and outsiders alike into my experiences. I set into motion a continuum of resonance or dissonance, seeking 'to produce aesthetic and evocative thick descriptions of personal and interpersonal experience' (Ellis et al. 2011: 277). The intention is not only to make personal experience meaningful and cultural experience engaging. By producing accessible texts, I may be able to reach wider and more diverse mass audiences that traditional research usually disregards (Ellis et al., 2011). The autoethnography is not simply about laying bare personal experiences, pains, or traumas, it is about inviting readers into a particular reality which might awaken in them points of identification, familiarity; a sense, perhaps, of giving words to similar experiences.

Importantly, I am not seeking validation, approval, assurance, or vengeance. Although, of course, it might be possible for readers to feel a resonance, a sense-making, even validation by reading their own experiences in mine. In one sense, therefore, I am reclaiming my own story, not through the theorised conjecture of others, but through my own memories and witnessing. In another sense, I am countering and disrupting conventional approaches to research, which persist in claiming that research is somehow neutral and impersonal, and that it is possible for a researcher to stand outside of her research. To Ellis et al. (2011: 274), 'autoethnography is one of the approaches that acknowledges and accommodates subjectivity, emotionality, and the researcher's influence on research, rather than hiding from these matters or assuming they don't exist'. In this regard, autoethnography offers an expansive lens on the world, steering away from rigid definitions of what constitutes meaningful and useful research (Ellis et al., 2011). This view is echoed by Pillay et al. (2016: 8), who maintain that 'It is in finding imaginative ways to communicate our insights with other people that these insights deepen and broaden, while simultaneously inviting responses from others.'

In yet another sense, by inviting readers into the realm of my personal experiences, I hope to awaken and sensitise readers to issues of identity politics, and to forms of representation that deepen our capacity to empathise with people who are different from us (Ellis & Bochner, 2000). I am initiating and opening gateways to conversations, ordinarily not had, at least not in an academic domain where canonical texts and ideas have long only captured a 'white', male perspective. I see my writing as a form of activism against hegemonic patterns of disempowering interpretations of the proverbial 'other'. I am interested not only in making my experiences known, but in entering new kinds of conversations with all 'others'. I am interested in changing a world, which thinks it already knows me, and therefore seeks to contain and control me and all 'others', and hence, fall outside the centres of power.

As to be expected, autoethnography is not without its criticisms. Commonly, it is dismissed as being insufficiently rigorous, theoretical and analytical, and too aesthetic, emotional and therapeutic; for conducting too little fieldwork; for observing too few cultural members; for not spending enough time with (different) 'others'; and for not fulfilling scholarly obligations of hypothesising, analysing and theorising (Delamont, 2009; Ellis et al., 2011). Seemingly, however, all these criticisms depart from the very same binary understanding, which autoethnography seeks to disrupt. Autoethnography does not conceive of science and art as two separate phenomena or processes. As human beings, we are as constitutive of rational thought and scientific thinking, as we are of emotions and intuition. Research is seldom empty of emotive drives to seek clarity and understanding. As researchers, we are motivated by social, societal and, in my case, educational dilemmas, and questions. These problems necessarily stem from and lead to our condition as human beings, making it impossible to extract the aesthetic or the emotive from how we engage in this world. It is possible, therefore, as expressed through an autoethnographic approach, for research to be rigorous, theoretical and analytical, as well as emotional, therapeutic and inclusive of personal and social phenomena (Ellis et al., 2011). For autoethnographers, argues Holman Jones (2005), research and writing are socially-just acts; the goal is to produce analytical, accessible texts that change us and the world we live in for the better.

The centrality of the self is both the strongest and weakest point of the autoethnography. While strength resides in the personalisation, intimacy and accessibility of lived experiences, the arising weakness stems from the very vulnerability implicit within this kind of approach. Autoethnography demands a particular kind of integrity and exposure, which, once revealed and captured in writing, cannot be retracted. At play are complexities of vulnerabilities – not only in the author removing her veils, but in having no way of knowing how the writing will be received or interpreted. Will the writing be received with empathy and sensitivity, or with hostility and rejection? The intention might be to break the mould of unspoken conversations and realities, the outcome might be quite different. There is no guarantee (not that there ever is in research) that readers will see what the author desires for them to see. In turn, by implication, an autoethnography exposes those around the author. My story inevitably implicates others and their roles, without me necessarily being able to safeguard their identities. My story cannot be told as if it unfolded in isolation or in a vacuum; my story is always connected with and to others. In fact, sometimes the story only exists *because* of others.

Hence, although the autoethnography might foreground the perspective of an individual, the individual cannot be de-situated. The production of theory is influenced by various factors, which means, says Haraway (1988: 581), that knowledge is always 'situated'. In this way, the story that is told is always reflective of a particular milieu and becomes the research context of the author.

To Anderson (2006), autoethnography extends beyond postmodern research which blurs the boundaries between the objective and the subjective, to erasing the objective and subjective binary, thereby collapsing the observer and subject into each other. Consequently, explain Ellis et al. (2011), when applied to autoethnography, the context, meaning and utility of terms such as 'reliability', 'validity', and 'generalisability' are altered. While issues of reliability hinge on the author or narrator's credibility, validity relies on whether the experiences described are believable and coherent (Ellis et al., 2011). The focus of generalisability resides with the readers – it is up to them to decide whether a story speaks to them or matters to them.

Adding to these complexities, is the risk that autoethnography entrenches an individualist strain innate to the liberal narrative or tradition. Alvesson (2003) describes autoethnography as 'too inward looking'. In turn, Delamont (2009: 51) refers to it as 'an intellectual cul de sac', with the problems being examined as mere forms of self-obsession, devoid of analytical quality. To her, 'autoethnography is antithetical to the progress of social science because it violates the two basic tasks of the social sciences, which are: to study the social world and to move their discipline forward' (Delamont, 2009: 60). And yet, as I set out to show in the ensuing discussion as well as the rest of this book, autoethnography, if approached with the necessary ethical caution, can advance social and societal dilemmas in ways that empirical or ethnographic studies never could. I think we can all agree that there are specific experiences that can only be conveyed from an insider perspective. I think we can also agree that this insider status is especially valuable to minority and marginalised groups, who have long been spoken on behalf of, or over (see Nel et al., 2019; Tewolde, 2020). The very society we are all seemingly intent on advancing and improving has hitherto been largely complicit in valuing certain voices and forms of knowledge of others.

The foregrounding of my own story is neither a propagation of the 'I' as an individualistic endeavour, nor a minimising of the 'I's' of others. The 'I' is always already situated in a particular socio-politico-cultural context, thereby connecting the individual identity to a collective one. To Poerwandari (2021), the power of autoethnography arises from the depth of experience or empirical data being shared, conceptual insight and analysis, as well as its ability to evoke reflexive insight for the readers. Realising what is experienced and accepting it as something to be learnt, is not easy, contends Poerwandari (2021: 317), 'Autoethnography becomes the embodiment of epistemology of practice and reflective practice'. Critical reflection, she continues can be conducted by deconstructing, confronting, theorising, or challenging oneself to think differently from the dominant frames of thinking to find better ways of thinking and practice (Poerwandari, 2021). In this way, autoethnography offers a critical counter-narrative, allowing marginalised and excluded individuals to speak for themselves. This is not an easy undertaking; it requires a willingness to resist canonised norms as well as values. This willingness is not tied to a singular desire to make my story known, it is embedded in sharing the untold experiences of minority and marginalised communities, with the hope of contributing to a more socially just world.

While autoethnography provides me with a unique philosophical orientation through which to tell my story, I am less confident about the capacity of feminism to capture the lived experiences of a Muslim woman, resident in a 'third world' context. In this regard, as I will try to highlight in the ensuing discussions, there are several concerns with the dominating presumption and conjecture which pervade feminism. Not only does feminism presuppose a systematic silencing of women, imposed through a systemic pattern of power and authority, but it presumes that the silencing is unjust and that there are ways of remedying this injustice (Lugones & Spelman, 1983).

Postcolonial experiences 'from below'

Mohanty (1984: 334) notes that despite Western feminist discourse and political practice being neither singular nor homogeneous in its goals, interests, or analyses, it is still possible to trace a coherence of effects resulting from the implicit assumption of 'the West' (in all its complexities and contradictions) as the primary referent in theory and praxis. Although Western feminism is not carved in stone, it is possible, Mohanty (1984: 334) asserts, to 'draw attention to the similar effects of various textual strategies used by particular writers that codify 'others' as non-Western and hence themselves as (implicitly) Western'. It is presumed, following Lugones and Spelman (1983: 575), 'that those who do the theory know more about those who are theorised than vice versa: hence it ought to be the case that if it is white/Anglo women who write for and about all other women, then white/Anglo women must know more about all other women than other women know about them'.

The irony, however, is that 'black' and colonised women know a lot more about 'white' women and the impositions of Anglo-normativity, than is the case conversely. 'Black' women come into the lives and homes of 'white' women in a way that 'white' women never do or need to do. Practices of this 'coming in' adopt any number of forms – from cleaning homes to the more sacred enclave of child-rearing, perhaps, most uniquely and paradoxically captured in a South African image of a 'white' child tied to the back of a 'black' woman. Though attached to *her* back, and reared through *her* tongue, the 'white' child must acquire the ways of the 'white' mother, which means that the 'black' woman cannot only be 'black'. To fulfil her role in the 'white' home, she has to adopt 'white' ways, etiquette and norms. This, however, is not to say that she *is* 'white'. She remains 'black', which is why she fulfils these subservient surrogate roles in the first place. While intimate, the relationship sits in a precarious enactment of trust – precarious, mostly because of the unequal balance of knowledge. While 'black' women know a lot more about what 'white' women's lives look like, the same cannot be said about 'white' women regarding the lives of 'black' women. In most cases, the closest 'white' women get to the lives of 'black' women is at the meeting or drop-off points of the nearest train station or bus terminus.

Colonialism not only ensured that the colonised adopts the

language, clothing, education and traditions of the coloniser, but its disdain for the ways and voices of the colonised is evident in its attempts (and successes) of erasure, rendering such lives as irrelevant and negligible. The 'brute facts' according to Lugones and Spelman (1983: 575) are that 'white'/Anglo women are 'ill at ease' in the world of the colonised 'in a very different way' than the colonised are 'ill at ease' in theirs. Neither is of each other's worlds. If they are to make a living for themselves and their families, then colonised women are required to adopt and embody the ways of 'white'/Anglo women; their own ways are a priori value-less. Their place in the world is not determined by them. This is because the world in which they find themselves – at least in colonised as well as patriarchal societies – is already determined on their behalf, regulated by prescribed norms and expectations. Significantly, the nature of the differences or schisms which separate the lives of women, is entirely relational. Middle-class women can live the lives they do precisely because working-class 'white', 'black' and Latina women live the lives they do (Barkley Brown, 2006).

For the most part, Western feminism has not taken account of the deeply pained voices and experiences born on the wrong side of systemic and structural hegemonies. Not only has Western feminism emerged from a relatively small pool of women, but it has been quick to delineate the voices of these women from the voices of 'others'. This delineation has taken effect in 'third world' feminist theory, which holds that feminist theories from the 'West' have failed to be relevant to the lives of women who are not 'white' or middle class (Lugones & Spelman, 1983).

The connection between 'others' or 'third world' women (as a category of homogenous oppression) 'as historical subjects and the re-presentation of Woman produced by hegemonic discourses is not a relation of direct identity, or a relation of correspondence or simple implication', asserts Mohanty (1984: 334). Rather, she contends, it is 'an arbitrary relation set up by particular cultures … [that] discursively colonise the material and historical heterogeneities of the lives of women in the third world, thereby producing/re-presenting a composite, singular "Third World Woman" – an image which appears arbitrarily constructed, but never carries with it the authorising signature of Western humanist discourse' (Mohanty, 1984: 334–335). As a result, while 'Western feminists' become the 'true subjects' of a counter-history and narrative, 'third world' women never rise above their generality and their 'object' status:

> [T]hird world women as a group or category are automatically and necessarily defined as: religious (read 'not progressive'), family-oriented (read 'traditional'), legal minors (read 'they-are-still-not-conscious-of-their-rights'), illiterate (read 'ignorant'), domestic (read 'backward') and sometimes revolutionary (read 'their-country-is-in-a-state-of-war-they-must-fight!'). This is how the 'third world difference' is produced. (Mohanty, 1984: 351–352)

The agency (centre) claimed by Western feminism operates in a dyadic relationship to the passivity (periphery) of 'third world' feminism. The establishment of the 'third world' as economically impoverished and dependent is juxtaposed against the political, social and economic advancement of the 'first world'. Seemingly, without this relational construction, neither the 'first world', nor the privileged positioning of Western women is enabled. Stated differently, the hierarchical positioning 'first world' or Western women is sustained through a subjugated representation of 'third world' women. This centre is maintained not only by who controls the narrative, and in which direction the narrative is allowed to go, but it leaves 'third world' feminist discourses to either defend or contest their peripheral position (Mohanty, 1984).

It is unclear whether the passivity, helplessness and repression, generally ascribed to 'third world' women arise because of their peripheral liminality, or whether their liminality is because of their perceived passivity. Regardless of how this seemingly dyadic relationship unfolds, the discursive discourse accompanying marginalisation remains the same – that of disempowerment and subjugation. What is apparent is that arguments propagated by voices from the centre, suggest impenetrable concentric lines between themselves and 'others' – thereby, preserving the dominance of Western feminism, on the one hand, and the continuing misrepresentation of 'other' women, on the other hand. In the end, first, Western feminist theory is implicitly and explicitly directed at the advancement of Western whiteness, entrenching hierarchies of racial, social and economic oppression. Second, when Western feminism appropriates the experiences of non-'white' and non-Western women to support arguments which seek only to better their own position, they, in fact, participate in discursive colonisation (Mohanty, 1988).

One of the foremost risks of discursive colonisation is that it designates 'third world' women, or the gendered subaltern to a position without identity, one 'where social lines of mobility, being elsewhere, do not permit the formation of a recognizable basis of action' (Spivak, 2005: 476). Understood in this way, women who look like me, can neither think, nor speak for themselves; they can only be spoken on behalf of. In my presence, I am absent. In my speech, I am not heard. To Spivak (1988), the gendered subaltern cannot speak, not because women do not have a voice or will not act, but because she is not given a subject-position from which to speak or act. Depending on my context, different markers – my race, or my identity as a Muslim woman – function as my essential and unreachable difference, a difference so unrecognisable, and outside of the centre, that I cannot be trusted to (re)present that difference. In turn, the more I am spoken about, or on behalf of, the more my subjugated status is re-institutionalised, and the more hegemonic systems of speech, action and theory are reproduced.

Recognising that there are lived experiences and voices on the outside, below structures and systems of power, necessitates a reconsideration of feminism and its espousal of theories. Feminist theories are not just about what happens to the female population in any given society or across all societies. Islamic feminism, for example, emerged as a new discourse or interpretation of Islam and gender, based on 'ijtihād [independent analysis] of the Qur'an and other religious texts' (Badran, 2009: 2). Badran (2009) explains that Islamic feminism is not simply a reform of religion and society; it is a fundamental alteration towards an egalitarian Islam, which does not locate the spheres of public and private on opposite ends of a continuum. In this way, feminist theories, contend Lugones and Spelman (1983: 576–577), 'are about the meaning of those experiences in the lives of women. They are about beings who give their own accounts of what is happening to them or of what they are doing, who have culturally constructed ways of reflecting on their lives'. In this sense, 'the concept of a woman's voice is itself a theoretical concept' (Lugones & Spelman, 1983: 574). When I give voice to my own existence and lived experiences, I become the theory. What emerges is a synthesis, not always orderly, at times, even messy and chaotic, but the theory of who I am lives in the fusion of the intersections of my identity. The messiness and chaos emanate from the way I have learnt to navigate my worlds, what to foreground, what to play down, what to speak about, when to remain silent. I am intensely conscious of what Matsuda (1992: 2) describes as a 'multiple consciousness', not only as a 'constant shifting of consciousness', but as 'the search for the pathway to a just world' (1992: 3). The category of Muslim women, for instance, is not fixed. Muslim women are not defined by a common identity, or by a common understanding of Qur'anic exegeses. As Kirmani (2009: 49) points out, Muslim women carry with them multiple intertwined identities; the expressions of their identities and practices are connected to and shaped by their own personal narratives and experiences.

As a 'coloured', Muslim woman, my experiences of both conscious and unconscious biases and prejudices are seldom singular. It is unclear whether the pauses of scrutiny I am often subjected to, arise from my skin colour (as might be the case in certain public settings), or religious identity (as might be the case at airports) or gender (as might be the case at certain religious gatherings or in specific religious spaces). I expand on all of these awkward experiences throughout this book. Suffice to say for now, it is hard to discern, at times, whether the discriminations I continue to experience are because of my gender, my race, or my religious identity, or whether, indeed, it is the combined effect of these multiple identities. I, therefore, cannot rely on feminism as my only theoretical lens. Its subversion of me and women like me, renders it as an untrustworthy optic. Instead, I turn to critical race feminism.

As an analytical tool, critical race feminism en-frames my lived experiences, while simultaneously allowing me to interrogate the intersectionality of my discriminatory experience. Originally coined by Richard Delgado, critical race feminism draws upon critical race theory, critical legal studies and 'black' feminist thought (Delgado & Stefanicic, 1995). Wing (2003: 1) describes critical race feminism as 'an embryonic effort in legal academia' to highlight the legal concerns of a significant group of people, who are routinely marginalised – 'those who are both women and members of today's racial/ethnic minorities, as well as disproportionately poor'. To Wing (2003), critical race feminism brings into question that there is an essential female voice – namely, that all women feel one way on a subject. Critical race feminism 'constitutes a race intervention in feminist discourse, in that it necessarily embraces feminism's emphasis on gender oppression within a system of patriarchy' (Wing, 2003: 7).

The pull of critical race feminism is that it provides a vehicle not only for critical analysis, but it serves as a living entity in which scholars (like me), can situate themselves to narrate their own experiences (Wing, 2003). This is appealing in more ways than one. As a living entity, critical race feminism recognises the embedded spaces of struggles, which necessarily precede, determine and follow the lives of women who are not 'white'. Yet, as I have already clarified in the first chapter, it does not exempt my perspectives and arguments from the same kind of critique on which I have and will continue to embark. This, as I will show through my writing, is the essence of transformative writing – while grounded in spaces of uncertainty, fear, struggle and oppression, it refuses to succumb to the impositions of others, it refuses to concede to the will of others, or the perpetual insertion of authority. As I embark on the experience of this book, I cannot shake the feeling that it is time to come home – home to who I am.

3

Race as disqualifying disfigurement

Futile efforts to dismiss allegations of racism are often followed by concessions that race is complex, and hence not easily definable. Whether explained as a sociohistorical process and construct, or a biological foundation, up to the 19th century, race was informed by essentialism. That is, the idea, says Appiah (2015: 3), 'that human groups have core properties in common that explain not just their shared superficial appearances but also the deep tendencies of their moral and cultural lives'. On the one hand, racial categorisation accommodates the scientific grouping of people. On the other hand, race is used to assign inherited moral and psychological tendencies, and to explain different histories and cultures of people (Appiah, 2015). For my own understanding of race, I rely on Yancy's (Peters, 2019: 663) conceptualisation of race as a 'social kind'. To Yancy, the concept of race does not have a referent in the natural world – 'There is no *thing* to which the concept of race points. So, it is a concept that is ontologically empty. Yet, it is a concept that exists. Its emergence in the world came from Western Europe. It is a concept that is socially and historically produced and shaped by colonial desire, bad faith, domination, psychological projection, and ontological and epistemic logics that are Manichean in nature' (Peters, 2019: 663).

The issue of race is ubiquitous to my story. It sits in every context and engagement – its presence dimmed only, at times, by other nodes of marginalisation. The colour of my skin is a source of contention not only in my own country, in which I am categorised as 'coloured', but in other localities for which there is no equivalent to a 'coloured' category'. It helps to explain that as a 'coloured' I have been reduced to neither 'black' nor 'white'. What I am is 'not'. The burden of a 'coloured' identity precedes apartheid; it emanates from a historical inheritance of colonialism, assigned to people from a mixed ancestry of European and African (and later Asian). The burden sits not only in the weight of a dehumanising racial classification, but in its distorted connotations of impurity and illegitimacy, designating yet another brutalisation of identity.

My decision to ponder on race in this chapter, as a foundationally consistent discrimination, ties into the awakening of my journey as an oppressed human being in my birthplace. It was the first kind of oppression I had experienced, and until a certain age in my life, I foolishly thought it would be the only kind of oppression I would experience. My initiation into the teaching profession would signal the first of many forceful realisations about how race works, penetrates and permeates even the most subtle forms of human engagement. In a very warped way, apartheid helped to easily demarcate and identify the structures and systems of racism. When these structures were removed, it became hard (at the time) not to recognise that racism is not in need of formalised legislation. In fact, it is the absence of formalised regulations which forces racism to live in masqueraded forms, assigning to it an even more dangerous obscenity and harm.

She thought I was at the wrong school

It was on a Monday morning in 1993 (nine months before South Africa would become a democratic state) – possibly early July – I cannot be certain, but it must have taken place as learners returned to school from their June holiday. It was a cold morning. Traffic from my home to Protea High School, located in the city centre of Cape Town was not only gruelling, but meant waking up extra early to get to school by 7:30.[2] My father had insisted on driving me – an insistence driven in part by amusement and in part by anxiety. I had tried to change the school at which I was meant to complete my teaching practical, but my Afrikaans lecturer had assured me that I was meant to be placed at a school which offered Afrikaans as a home language subject – given that my two teaching specialisations were English and Afrikaans. As I stepped out of the car, right in front of the entrance gate to the school, my father joked that there was still time to make a run for it. A joke I wished I had acted upon the moment the school secretary set her eyes on me.

After learning that I was a student teacher, she promptly informed me that I must be at the wrong school. Protea, she declared, did not accommodate students from the University of the Western Cape (UWC). Her choice of words offered her a deft way of telling me that the school did not accommodate 'coloured' or 'black' student teachers. It is useful to know that when UWC was initially established in 1959, it was named the University College of the Western Cape as a constituent college of the University of South Africa for people classified as 'coloured'. The first group of 166 students enrolled in 1960. They were offered limited training for lower to middle-level positions in schools, the civil service and other institutions designed to serve a separated 'coloured' community. In 1970, the institution gained university status and was able to award its own degrees and diplomas.

---

2   Protea High School is a pseudonym.

My confused face became her bewilderment, as she processed my response that I was not from UWC, but from the University of Cape Town (UCT). She took her processing behind closed doors, as she mumbled something about having to speak to the principal. I stood waiting, until the man, identified as my mentor-teacher, arrived. He carried himself with a look that suggested either indifference or boredom. Either he had been forewarned by the presence of a 'coloured' student teacher waiting in the foyer, or he simply could not care, as he ushered me into the staffroom, just in time for morning briefings. At the time, I neither had the insights, nor the language to grasp that one of the most debilitating aspects of being seen in terms of my racially prescribed identity – regardless of whether I believe in it or not – is that I am constantly compelled to address my imposed exclusion before I can participate in whatever space I find myself. That morning at Protea was no different, as I anxiously tried to assess where and how to situate myself in a space that was not meant to accommodate someone like me.

The cold winter's day did little to relieve my increasingly flushed condition, as my mentor-teacher told me to follow him to *saal* (assembly). I was told to sit in the gallery. *Saal* was a carefully orchestrated affair, involving a procession of learners carrying the (old) South African flag, followed by the *dominee* (pastor) and the principal, and the rest of the staff. Proceedings opened with the singing of the *Nasionale Stem* (old national anthem), and then a few words by the *dominee*. Everything about all of this, while perfectly normal in the world of Protea High School, made everything about me more abnormal. I was surrounded by the very symbols (the flag and the anthem), I had been protesting. My sense of being out-of-place was outweighed only by a dreaded sense of self-betrayal.

Matters became exceedingly absurd as my mentor-teacher mentioned that one of the learners in the class I would be teaching is the grandson of BJ (Balthazer Johannes, or John) Vorster. Vorster served as the prime minister of apartheid South Africa from 1966 to 1978, and then as its president from 1978 until 1979, when he was forced to resign due to the 'Information Scandal', also nicknamed 'Muldergate', in reference to Cornelius Petrus (Connie) Mulder who was the Minister of Information at the time. The Information Scandal was a result of government attempts to influence international and local public opinion about the apartheid government. The government embarked on a propaganda war. It shifted about R64 million from the defence budget to undertake a series of propaganda projects, which included bribing international news agencies, purchasing the *Washington Star* newspaper, and the secret establishment of a government-controlled newspaper, *The Citizen* – a newspaper that became influential in the formation of English public opinion.

I am not sure why my mentor-teacher felt the need to point out the presence of Vorster's grandson to me – perhaps, he too, noticed the profound irony of a 'coloured' (Muslim) student teacher teaching the bloodline of not only an apartheid prime minister and president, but one of the founding members of the *Ossewa-Brandwag* (ox-wagon sentinel). The *Ossewa-Brandwag*, established in 1939, was an anti-British and pro-German organisation in South Africa during the Second World War and which opposed South African participation in the war. During the early years of World War II Vorster became a general of its paramilitary wing, known as the *Stormjaers* (the Stormtroopers), which was modelled on the Nazi *Sturmabteilung* (the Storm Division or Brown Shirts).

Other than being designated as a place for teaching and learning, nothing about the school made me feel comfortable. There were two other student teachers at the school. I knew both from my Higher Diploma in Education (HDE) class. They, however, did not suffer the same uncertainty of placement or recognition that I did. Their entries into the staff room, or the school foyer did not elicit the same kind of tense confusion that mine did. While they looked the part of a teacher at a historically 'white' school, I did not. The frustration and anxiety of the first few days were distressful enough for me to request a placement at another school. I felt compromised and let down. What was my Afrikaans lecturer thinking in placing me at a school that symbolised the epiphany of Afrikanerdom? Everything about the school resonated with a propagation of apartheid. What was I supposed to learn in a school like this? My complaints to my lecturer fell on deaf ears. He felt confident about his decision, as well as his opinion that I would gain much from the experience. His confidence did not do much for me. But I knew that I needed to find a way to get through the next six weeks, which was the duration of the teaching practical during the second semester. The previous one, during the first semester, I had spent at a 'coloured' school.

Each day felt like a mountain to climb. Most of my time centred on me trying not to draw attention to myself. I was petrified of being 'too visible', as if someone would suddenly realise, 'hey, she's not white!' My interaction with teachers at the school was limited to that with my mentor–teacher. While always very busy, he was great at offering advice. My time in the staff-room was spent with my head down. While the other two students enjoyed making coffee and chatting in the kitchen, I dared not enter. It was one thing to enter a professional space as an 'unknown', and presumably, 'unwelcome' intrusion. It was quite another to assume the privilege of sharing in kitchen utensils. It was not just that I had no place at the school. My presence, while surreal to some, like the secretary, was indeed a physical one, and it signalled something much bigger than me. I was a sign of change. It was 1993. I was evidence that apartheid was facing an uncertain future.

I managed to get through those six weeks for only one reason: the learners. Whether because of their youth, or whether my status as a 'teacher' afforded me authority, which could not be defied, none of them were ever disrespectful to me. In fact, I was amazed by their exceptionally polite conduct – from greeting and thanking me for lessons, to jumping from the seats to find chalk whenever I ran short.

Off to another wrong school

As my HDE year was ending, I had the option of at least three teaching posts. While two were at 'coloured' schools, one was at a 'white' school. The country was preparing for its first democratic elections; schools had already begun to slowly desegregate in preparation for the inevitability of an apartheid-free society. My discomfort at Protea was not yet a distant memory, but I also knew that something in me had changed, hence my careful consideration of a post at a soon to be 'historically white' school. The experience had indeed given me a valuable lesson – that teaching and being a teacher is about learning, and hence, learners. I felt emboldened, ready to become a part of the country's transition into a new period and milieu of enveloping diversity.

The hopeful acceptance of my first teaching post during the most momentous year of South Africa's history lasted until I reported for my first day of duty. Unsurprisingly, I encountered the same secretary at the school of my first teaching post in January 1994. Not the same person, but the same persona – the kind who spent most of her interactions with me in carefully worded efforts of reminding me to know my place. In an unwavering tone of condescension, she would find it necessary to remind me about school rules, where and where not to place files, how to make appointments to speak to the principal. While painfully efficient in her assertion of authority over me, she would 'forget' to relay messages regarding the cancellation of sports events, or the re-scheduling of meetings. She was more than prepared to assist learners when sent by other ('white') teachers when they needed copies made or required stationery. Any learner sent by me, would return with a terse message that she was out of stock, or that I should fetch it myself during break. Her face was a constant contortion of horror and disgust if not at the influx of 'coloured' learners into what was an exclusively 'white' school just a year before, then at what she clearly perceived as the audaciously intrusive presence of the three newly appointed 'coloured' teachers, of which I had the privilege/misfortune of being one.

On the surface, there was a sense of widening expectation and aspiration, a hope for an end to human suffering. It was hard not to get caught in the romance of it all, to be part of such a profound part of history. I was a part of this – the euphoric witnessing of the end of apartheid, as well as the history leading to it. I had been forced out of my childhood home when I was thirteen years old. By that same time my father had already experienced forced removals, implemented under what was known as the Group Areas Act (Act no. 41 of 1950), twice over. Thousands of people had lost their lives – if not to death, then in conditions of existence that could not be described as living. It is hard to thread words through certain experiences. It is hard to capture what it means to experience not being seen as human, but as something else, perhaps a mistake in colour. The violence inflicted on bodies, who were not 'white', lived in many forms and spaces. It is easy to name the violence of dehumanising oppression, it is quite another when it lives in who you are perceived to be. Das (2007: 9) explains that it is not only the violence experienced on an individual's body, 'but also the sense that one's access to context is lost that constitutes a sense of being violated'. Hence, even in the elation and pride of a momentous political accomplishment, I understood that a democracy could not erase the violence – not in those who suffered it, and not in those who perpetrated it.

If I thought that my time as a student had in any way prepared me for what was to come in my first year of teaching, I was wrong. I had naively thought that the ideological displacement I had experienced at Protea High School would somehow equip, even buffer me against the kinds of unease, marginalisation and invisibility of any similar kind of setting. I have subsequently learnt and lived that even when contexts *look* the same – whether in terms of historical disposition, or teacher and learner demographics – contexts are never the same. Difference emanates not only from different ways of acting and being, but from what those actions and beings evoke and provoke in others. All the pedagogical knowledge, skills and readiness could not prepare me for what awaited me in my first teaching position. Like Protea High, Erica High School[3] was reserved for 'white' learners

---

3   Erica High School is a pseudonym.

and teachers only. But the year in which I started teaching was in 1994, which coincided with South Africa's transition to a democracy, and hence, the accompanying desegregation of schools. Given the nascency of this transition at the time, most of the learners in my classes were 'white'. It was quite an absurd situation when one considers that I was teaching learners from the very background with whom I had not been allowed to learn.

The way he turned his back shortly after being introduced to me by the principal suggested that he had no interest in seeing or getting to know me. All ensuing communication between us relied on the least amount of eye contact possible. I would be lying if I said we ever had a conversation or interaction. He did not interact with me; that would imply some sort of inter-relation, or that he deemed me as someone with a voice. The fact that he was the head of the Afrikaans department gave him the unnecessary power he so deeply enjoyed wielding over me. The unannounced classroom visits were as demoralising as his unintelligent instructions that I remove visual images from the grade 8 examination paper, or that I only choose creative writing topics from his approved list. My attempts at any sort of contribution to the Afrikaans department was his cue to dismiss me and my ideas. While the other five 'white' teachers actively participated and took the lead in designing materials for the different grades, I was treated like someone who had no understanding of my subject specialisation or teaching. He must have spent endless hours re-marking entire sets of examination scripts, when all he should have been doing was moderate a few. He even went as far as questioning the high marks of learners, raising doubt about my 'standard of teaching', even when they were 'white', just because they were taught by me. He made no attempt to hide the fact that he did not approve of me. These were my experiences in 1994. Seemingly, the use of 'standards' continues to be deployed as a distinction between 'white' competence and 'black' incompetence (see Jansen, 2004; Soudien & Sayed, 2004; Walker, 2005; Davids, 2019a).

The head of the Afrikaans department was also in charge of the book-room, where all the textbooks were stored. He carried the seriousness of this responsibility around his neck in the form of a key, which he would hand over with painfully clear instructions that teachers only take the requested books, and not untidy the book-room. Since I was never given the privilege of being handed the key, I (thankfully) escaped any potential accusations of untidying the book-room. I could not be trusted to identify and take the books which I needed, which meant that I was always accompanied by him. I remember laughing at myself for thinking that had I taught any other subject, but languages, my trips to the book-room might have been limited to no more than twice a year – once at the beginning of the year to collect the books, and again at the end of the year, to return them. The fact that I taught English and Afrikaans, meant collecting and returning various sets of novels, plays, poetry anthologies, as well as grammar textbooks throughout the year. That this mindless act would come to warrant so much attention in my life says something about my dreaded interactions with this man. It must have been exhausting for him – feeling compelled to manage me all the time, always suspicious, always waiting. By the time I left the school four years later, I had begun pitying him, his blinkered and entrapped thinking, the simmering frustration and resentment of witnessing apartheid slowly oozing away.

It certainly did not help matters that during my first year I had completed co-authoring an Afrikaans textbook, *Kaperjol*. I had been invited to be part of this collaborative effort on the recommendation of my Afrikaans lecturer during my pre-service teaching year. There was a dire need for an abandonment of the old textbooks (in most subjects), not only because of its outdated content, but for its racist overtones. The publication of the textbook coincided with the introduction of the country's new outcomes-based curriculum, and as such, offered a fresh take on content and teaching approaches, reflective of an inclusive democratic society. It was an exciting project, working with different and more experienced teachers, curriculum experts and copy-editors, and I was incredibly proud just to be included as an author. While most of the schools in the province and country opted to prescribe *Kaperjol*, my school did not – even when I indicated that as an author I could secure a generous discount. Instead, the head of the Afrikaans department insisted that the school continues to use the same textbooks used during apartheid and made it clear that he had no interest in implementing the new nationally prescribed curriculum. As I reflect upon him now, I almost admire his unabashed racism: he knew who he was and what he stood for and had no qualms in making sure that, in his eyes, I know what I did or had to say simply did not matter. I am reminded of Ahmed's (2004) observation, that if we recognise something such as racism, then we also offer a definition of that which we recognise. To her, recognition produces rather than simply finds its object; recognition delineates the boundaries of what it recognises as given. Over the years, while working in different educational spaces, I would come to realise that in many ways it is easier to deal with this kind of brazenness than it is to be misled into the subtleties of facades of inauthentic interactions and conversations.

On most days, it was possible to compartmentalise and block out the actions and speech of the head of the Afrikaans department. Although I initially considered bringing up the matter with the principal, it became apparent that he might not necessarily be equipped to respond or deal with the situation. South Africa's newly 'opened' schools were as uncharted to him, as they were to all other school leaders. While generally cordial and highly professional, I seriously doubted his capacity to know how to respond to my allegations of racism. My initial interview with him when I had applied for the position was functional and brief. He called me later the same day to offer me the post. As a 'white' male, his lifeworld had ill-prepared him to understand or relate to the experiences of marginalisation and exclusion that naturally accompany the lives of oppressed and disenfranchised citizens in South Africa. So, instead, I threw myself into my teaching, my learners, their dramatic teenage angsts, which typify teenagers across the spectra of divisions, apartheid was so intent on safeguarding. Their youthful vigour and insatiable, energetic curiosity served as continuous confirmation that I belonged in teaching. Their diversity in terms of race, religion and culture, coupled with profound disparate historical contexts – enforced through apartheid legislation – made for unprecedented teaching and learning encounters and opportunities.

I thrived on it, even while suspecting that the vibrancy of a dramatically shifting political context might not be enough to counter or dilute the scars of an apartheid society. There were also wonderfully light moments, such as a phone call from a 'white' mother urgently wanting to speak to me about her sixteen-year-old daughter's blossoming romance with a 'coloured youngster'. My suspicions that she was unaware of my own 'coloured' identity were confirmed when I saw the expression on her face the next day. Her planned conversation rapidly changed to one on her daughter's academic progress – a somewhat redundant conversation, given that her daughter was the top learner in the grade. Her obvious awkward embarrassment aside, I was heartened to know that her daughter had either not mentioned the race of her class teacher, or her mother had forgotten or had become confused as to which teacher was the 'coloured' one. I could not know how much this realisation would impact on my teaching in later years – that is, that some learners or students simply see teachers as teachers; they are unbothered by race, religion, ethnicity or culture; they are only interested in your teaching.

By the end of my second year of teaching, the learner demographics had shifted radically from being an exclusively 'white' school to a predominantly 'coloured' one. Learner migration refers to the movement of learners from 'black' townships on the periphery of cities to former 'white', 'coloured' and 'Indian' schools situated in relatively more affluent areas (Pampallis, 2003). The abandonment of the Group Areas Act facilitated rapid migrations of families across racially designated residential areas. It is not just that communities in South Africa lived in separate areas, and hence did not interact.

It is that the measure of infrastructural and recreational support assigned to an area was determined by its racial occupation. Those designated to the lowest levels of 'blackness' received the least amount of service delivery, compounded by a deliberate attitude of indifference. The potential for post-apartheid migration is mostly defined by financial capacity. The desire to do so is based either on a nostalgic and restorative return to homes from which people were forcibly removed, or to live in environments that are habitable, safe and close to places of employment. The forced removals actioned through the Group Areas Act did not only expel people from family homes, it also displaced them into far-flung patches of land, devoid of communal living and recreational facilities, and far from the employment hub of the city centre.

The surrounding area of Erica High has historical associations of immense residential upheaval for 'coloured' communities. It also has connotations of a bustling middle-class community. The rapid change in residential demography was both accompanied and enabled by 'white' families opting to move to the 'northern suburbs', which were considered to be 'more white'. This perception is no longer the case. Moreover, the school is near a railway line, which was seen as expediting the influx of learners across racial lines. Seemingly, the more 'coloured' and 'black' learners accessed the school, the more 'white' learners exited, often in the direction of what was becoming an intense proliferation of private schools (including faith-based schools) in post-apartheid South Africa. With the scrapping of the Group Areas Act (no. 41 of 1950), similar contextual changes were unfolding in the surrounding residential areas. Communities previously prohibited from living in better resourced and serviced areas migrated from far-flung apartheid-erected areas. To some, this migration signalled a reclamation of historical dispossession. To others, financial mobility ensured a smooth facilitation into the gains of a democracy.

Despite the evident residential and demographic shifts that happened across South Africa in the early days of democracy, these shifts, relatively speaking, remain minimal. The historical disenfranchised situatedness of the overwhelming majority of 'black' and 'coloured' communities remain unchanged, regardless of widespread political and policy reform. Because of this contextual reality, the implied desegregation of newly 'opened' schools, is neither significant, nor representative of the myriad policy-suggested forms of integration. Although it is possible to discern definitive patterns of migration across historically racialised schools from 'black' to 'coloured' and 'Indian', and from 'black', 'coloured' and 'Indian' to 'white' schools, which have resulted, in some instances, in complete shifts in learner demographics at some schools, the actual number represents but a small slice of the overall learner pie (Woolman & Fleisch, 2006; McKinney, 2010). Furthermore, regardless of the immense diversity in terms of race, culture, ethnicity and language that clearly exists at several South African schools, these schools have not succeeded in creating and cultivating integrated learning and social spaces (Naidoo et al., 2018; Soudien & McKinney, 2016).

There are numerous and complex issues and tensions at play, some of which can be conceived of in terms of external exclusionary measures, and others that take shape through practices of internal exclusion. On the one hand, schools employ policies of charging exorbitant fees, select the language(s) of teaching and learning, and demarcate feeder zones to keep particular communities of learners at bay. The steady increase in school fees, for example, provides critical insights into the relationality between race and class, and how this serves to perpetuate inequalities (Davids, 2020).

Desegregation is still about race

First signs of the rumbling tension among teachers at Erica High reared at the beginning of 1995. South Africa had adopted its newly designed flag at the same time as the country's first democratic elections on 27 April 1994. The new flag, depicting colours of the South African Republic, the Union, as well as the African National

Congress, replaced the old flag which had been in use since 1928.

Generally, while historically 'white' schools proudly displayed the South African flag during apartheid, many were slow in adopting the new flag and its accompanying symbolism. Erica was one such school. Week after week, as we gathered for school assembly, I would cast my eye in the direction of the flag, still seeing the old one. By November of 1994, the only three 'coloured' staff members decided to raise the matter with the principal. He tried to minimise the significance of it and offered to discuss it at a meeting with senior staff members, which, by implication, excluded the three of us. I found his response perplexing, not only in his attempts to discount the flag as a symbol of 'white' supremacy, but in seemingly failing to see the necessity of replacing the old flag, in line with state regulations. Instead, he relied on the assertion that the old flag was not prohibited. Its illegality would only come into effect 25 years later, in 2019, when Judge Phineas Mojapelo ruled that any 'gratuitous' display of the old flag amounted to hate speech, racial discrimination and harassment under the Equality Act. In line with the thinking of anyone who comprehended the true state and experience of the apartheid regime's objectives, Judge Mojapelo ruled that:

> The dominant meaning attributable to the Old Flag, both domestically and internationally, is that it is for the majority of the South African population a symbol that immortalises the period of a system of racial segregation, racial oppression through apartheid, of a crime against humanity and of South Africa as an international pariah state that dehumanised the black population. (Ampofo-Anti, 2019)

Three weeks after our initial meeting, the principal informed the staff during a daily staff briefing, that after consulting with senior staff members, it was decided that both the new and old flag would be on display in the school hall, and at all formal ceremonies. This, to his mind, would represent a compromise between South Africa's history and present. There were three very unhappy staff members, none of whom were 'white'. I restated the argument made to him three weeks earlier that the old flag was a painful reminder to those who had suffered under apartheid; that it symbolised oppression and hatred; that, as a school community, we had a responsibility to cultivate a space where learners and teachers from diverse backgrounds could come together without the tensions induced by and presence of hateful symbols. As expected, my sentiments were not welcomed by most of my colleagues.

Others, like one of the history teachers, were at pains to explain that the old flag was a cherished symbol to 'white' Afrikaners, which, according to her, should not necessarily be equated with apartheid. She stressed that the views of the majority (of the staff) should be respected, apparently forgetting, or ignoring, the fact that the majority of the country had voted for the ANC, and a democracy, characterising severance with apartheid ideology and all of its symbols. Admittedly, I was more disheartened by the silences of ('white') colleagues, who previously had offered their support of the removal of the flag in private conversations with me, than with those who saw no problem in proudly displaying an apartheid symbol. If the principal thought that the annual school break three weeks later would somehow subdue the simmering tension, which had manifested from his announcement, he was wrong.

The new cohort of grade 8s in the new year saw a significant increase in the number of 'coloured' learners. Residential migratory patterns across historically segregated areas had a significant impact on school demographics in South Africa, forcing some of them to carefully recompose admission policies directed at keeping certain communities at bay – if not through race, then through finances. Proximity to major transport hubs or routes proved to be especially problematic for several historically 'white' schools. Ironically, the skewed privileging of effective transport systems in historically 'white' areas ensured easy access to those areas for members of communities who could not afford to relocate. Erica High could neither escape its rapidly changing residential base, nor its unfortunate proximity to a railway station.

By the time I resigned from my post early in 1998, the school was predominantly 'coloured', with a significant increase in 'black' learners. A change, such as this, is immediately accompanied by judgements of falling standards – the implicit contention being an association between quality and whiteness, as opposed to no-quality and blackness. Significantly, the predominance of the learner shift was not reflected in the staff demographics. Any new posts, at least during my tenure at the school, were exclusively filled by 'white' teachers. The new year also started with lines clearly drawn between the three 'coloured' staff members and the rest of the all-'white' staff. The issue of the flag had not been put to rest. I am not sure whether I would have arrived at the same decision to resign had I not taken maternity leave midway through all the tensions at school. I am also not certain of the extent to which the death of my father a mere week before the birth of my first daughter impacted me. I had planned to return, and I did for about three months, until one morning while driving to work, it suddenly dawned on me that I no longer wanted to be a part of this school.

There was a fractured-ness about the school. Collegial relationships had deteriorated into interactions of mistrust and unspoken frustrations. While emanating from a flag-dispute, the arising conflict laid bare unspoken experiences of racism, of not being seen as human beings, drawing hard lines between 'them' ('white' teachers) and 'us' ('coloured' teachers). Even in my moments of anger and disappointment, I recognised that most of the teachers and the principal simply did not understand what was often described as an 'unnecessary fuss'. After all, it was just a flag. So, what's the harm? It is not unusual to find an unwillingness on the part of certain teachers and school leaders to break from the past by persisting with practices that continue to be couched in a language of authoritarianism and alienation (Moloi, 2007; Ngcobo & Tikly, 2008). Matters reached a tipping point when after yet another assembly of having to sit on a stage with the old flag poised next to the new one, one of the teachers remarked that this was 'their school', and that if 'the "coloured" teachers did not like how things were done, they should leave'. I remember this statement as clearly as when I first heard it in the staffroom. I remember it because it led to such an unbearable staff atmosphere, that one of the 'coloured' teachers reported the matter to the district education department.

About two weeks later the staff was informed that we were required to attend a compulsory two-day conflict resolution session, mediated by a facilitator, appointed by the education department. Whether it was the fact that we had only two days, or the fact that the change in our society was just too new and raw, or whether my 'white' colleagues either did not want to care, or did not know how to care about what it meant to live as an oppressed person, or whether the facilitator was simply not equipped enough to adequately manage the volatility of the conflict, the session did not resolve anything. Sharing our perspectives had not only left both sides feeling emotionally exposed, but more intent upon and hardened in their own perspectives. Whatever facades of collegiality existed prior to the conflict resolution session had dissipated by the time we returned to the school.

As the antithesis of segregation, desegregation is meant to undo not only racial segregation, but the power, or in the case of South Africa, the law, which confers the separation. Apartheid saw the establishment of 19 racially and ethnically separated education departments. Not only would South Africa's children not learn together, but the racially differentiated funding allocation to 'white', 'Indian', 'coloured' and 'black' schools would ensure a foundation of educational, social and economic inequity – an imbalance critical to ensuring the success of the 'white' supremacist project, and a foundation that would extend long beyond the political demise of apartheid. Embodied in the Bantu Education Act of 1953 are the beliefs of apartheid architect, Hendrik Verwoerd, who maintained:

> There is no place for [the Bantu] in the European community above the level of certain forms of labour ... What is the use of teaching the Bantu child mathematics when it cannot use it in practice? That is quite absurd. Education must train people in accordance with their opportunities in life, according to the sphere in which they live. (McGregor 2013)

Ushered in by 'A Policy Framework for Education and Training' (DoE, 1994), public schools in South Africa embarked on a two-pronged process of curriculum renewal by replacing Christian National Education with an outcomes-based education and desegregation. While accompanied by much rhetoric of 'open schools' for all learners, the ideals of desegregation are far removed from what is practically possible within school contexts. Unlike desegregation in public spaces, such as restaurants or hotels, which might incur (temporary or permanent) economic losses, desegregation in schools, observes Howard Thurman (1966), attacks the foundations of society. Segregation does not only signal a regulation of access and participation, but it is also, says Thurman (1966), 'the exercise of raw power by one group of people over the lives of another group of people', ingrained and guaranteed by economic, political, social and religious sanctions. What desegregated schools imply, therefore, is the setting into motion of a new kind of society, where the privileging of one group and its interests are not privileged over another.

Desegregation in South Africa has not unfolded in ways that might have been envisaged. Presumably, there was some sort of expectation that all schools would suddenly be open to all learners. But how could this be? While promulgated by democratic principles, in practice, and in living, South African society remains deeply seeped in the residual dehumanisation of apartheid. So, no, all schools have become microcosms of the diversity which is South Africa. On the one hand, the majority of historically disenfranchised schools ('black', 'coloured' and 'Indian') have retained their 'disadvantaged' status. On the other hand, in most school contexts, where desegregation has occurred, it has been met with a combination of fear, suspicion and hostility, and untamed objectives to assimilate diversity into the dominant look and culture of the school (Davids, 2018b).

My short time at Erica High was tumultuous and unsettling. Sentimental notions of 'togetherness' and 'reconciliation', as espoused by Nelson Mandela, dissolved into shadows of suspicion and guardedness. Yet the pleasure I derived from my teaching and those I taught – regardless of race or ethnicity – was undeniable. I have never stopped cherishing the lives of the young people who touched mine during this time. The deeper the tensions among the staff, the more I sheltered in my classroom. Isolating myself became a means of self-preservation. By my third year at the school, the principal had resigned to take up a post at a private college. I was unsurprised; it had become increasingly hard for him to know how to lead and manage a diverse school, let alone know how to begin to respond to the obvious staff tensions and conflicts. It was clear to me that he had absolutely no point of reference from which to even begin to understand what it meant to live on the under-side of his oppression-free and privileged life.

From a broader perspective, informed by 27 years of so-called 'open schools' in democratic South Africa, I do not believe that principals, teachers, or policymakers, for that matter, had any idea of how to manage newly desegregated school spaces. In most cases, historically advantaged schools continue to be strained sites of racial tension and 'othering', fostering harmful and undignified experiences of worthlessness. Sites of harmful 'othering' and alienation. There is seemingly no shortage of racist vitriol, spewed by learners and teachers alike (Davids, 2018c; 2019c). My experiences of and at the school were certainly not unique; friends at other schools had similar, if not more disaffecting, experiences, resulting in several of them exiting the teaching profession altogether.

As in all cases, the decision to desegregate is a political one. The massive policy reform, which included the eventual iterations of four curricula over a 27-year period, never quite understood the criticality of attending to teachers and their identities in a post-apartheid climate. The government turned to Outcomes-Based Education (OBE) as a replacement for Christian National Education (CNE) – an education system (implemented in 1948) which was based on a particular Afrikaner form of Calvinistic principles. The massive curriculum overhaul took centre stage among the dissolution of nineteen different education departments, established during apartheid, directed at different racial and ethnic groups, and with different curricula. A new national curriculum for all South African learners was viewed as critical to cultivating a new democratic identity and citizenship. Instead of the authoritarian positioning of the teacher in CNE, OBE placed learners at the centre of their learning by encouraging their participation, and critical engagement. There was an overwhelming focus on getting the myriad of education policies right without asking the much-needed question of *who* is expected to implement the policies. Presumptions of a generic and abiding teacher were incredibly short-sighted. The prohibition of an apartheid system has not translated into an eradication of apartheid thinking or acting. I would, therefore, concur with Thurman (1966), that even if desegregation is facilitated by changes in policies and regulations, integration can never be achieved as an end but must emerge as an experience after the fact of coming together. South Africans have never had a chance to come together. Policies happened before we had a chance to know what it would be like to step out of residential, communal and political silos.

For some teachers, like those at Erica High, the leap of teaching only 'white' learners at the end of 1993, to having a diverse class six weeks later, was much more than some of their political leanings could tolerate. In the absence of acquiring a renewed understanding of a socially just society, one devoid of racism and its vile language, the only changes these teachers would have been capable of are the ones that they revealed – a forced preparedness to desegregate, but not to integrate. As explained by Judith Butler in an interview with George Yancy (2015: 8), 'Whiteness is less a property of skin than a social power reproducing its dominance in both explicit and implicit ways. When whiteness is a practice of superiority over minorities, it monopolises the power of destroying or demeaning bodies of colour.' Although desegregation can be legislated, integration cannot. Integration, as Thurman (1966) reminds us, requires an openness not only in terms of live options regarding all facilities, but is concerned with how we understand and come to our human relations.

Postcolonialism as a product of human experience

I don't think I fully comprehended the immense challenges South Africa faced as a post-apartheid society. I knew the effects of living during apartheid, followed by the unsettling experiences of crossing a literal colour line at Erica High. I knew the emotions of it, but I had no language through which to make sense of these experiences. Everything at the time was just too new, untraversed, and playing out against a political backdrop where reconciliation and hope seemingly loomed large. It would only be years later that I would begin to grasp the discursive entrenchment of the production and reproduction of existing hegemonies, such as those imposed by colonialism and apartheid. What does it mean for a society to transition into a postcolonial phase? For some, postcolonialism infers resistance to the colonial at any time – literally, asserts Young (2009), in the case of decolonised societies, and ideologically for still colonised societies. While Young (2009: 13) acknowledges that the term postcolonial will certainly always involve the idea of resistance, he prefers to 'preserve the historical specificity of the term, and to think of the postcolonial as involving what we might simply refer to as the aftermath of the colonial.' The aftermath, no doubt, is as wrapped up in the politics of transformation – such as the desegregation of schools – as it is, 'simply the product of human experience' (Young, 2009: 13).

If the aftermath of colonialism and apartheid lives on (and hides) in our human experiences, then it follows that we can only undo the aftermath through our experiences. If postcolonialism provides a language of and for those who seem not to belong, of those whose knowledges and histories are not allowed to count (Young, 2009), then it helps to use that language not only in making our experiences known, but in inviting others into our own experiences. In this regard, connected very closely to an autoethnographic approach, is the potential of storytelling to begin to deconstruct the estranged and vilified understandings apartheid succeeded in inculcating into South African society. The experiences described in this chapter are not historical; they are ever-present in our schools, where teachers relegated to minority group status continue to struggle for recognition as competent pedagogical authorities. The appointment of 'black' teachers at historically 'white' schools remains a painfully slow undertaking. Jansen (2007: 30) contends that incoming 'black' teachers 'are already framed in ways that disempower them, and the same nurturing and accommodation that is so readily made for novice 'white' teachers seldom apply to novice black teachers.' Spaces – the public sphere, schools and universities – acquire the 'skin' of the bodies that inhabit them; 'institutions' as orientation devices take the shape of 'what' resides within them (Ahmed, 2007: 157). When we describe institutions as 'being white' (institutional whiteness), explains Ahmed (2007: 157), 'we are pointing to how institutional spaces are shaped by the proximity of some bodies and not others: white bodies gather and cohere to form the edges of such spaces.'

The deployment of policies cannot reach the lived experiences of teachers or learners. Inasmuch as 'education is the construction and reconstruction of personal and social stories', so, too, teachers and learners are storytellers and characters in their own and other's stories (Connelly & Clandinin, 1990: 2). Neither teachers nor learners speak with one voice. There are some things that are true for some, but not so for others. There are ways of seeing the world, which are unseen to others. We are not fully of each other's worlds, which means that our intimacy is incomplete (Lugones & Spelman, 1983).

This is because, based on our pre-existing ideas and judgements of others, we reconstruct each other in the images or myths that we have of each other. But if we are to reconceive the way we engage with each other, learn how to be with each other and re-find each other in the aftermath, then we must cultivate spaces for us each to give account of ourselves. This is partly what makes us human – our capacity to articulate our experiences.

4

Parents (not) for Change

In terms of the South African Schools Act (no. 84 of 1996), the introduction of School Governing Bodies (SGBs) in South African schools is motivated by a democratic discourse of communal participation, belonging and accountability. The extant literature on governance in South African schools reveals a widening gap not only between the functionality of SGBs, but in the functionality of schools. In line with the dominant literature on school dysfunctionality, a similar focus has emerged on the incapacity of SGBs at historically disadvantaged schools. Consequently, very little attention has been given to 'functional' SGBs, especially when functionality is limited to the academic achievement of a school. Importantly, despite its democratising mandate, few questions are asked about the role of SGBs in relation to transformation and diversification.

The ensuing discussion focuses on my experiences as a member of a parent group, known as Parents for Change (PfC). The group emerged because of a series of events, which included the resignation of three parents from the SGB in August 2017. At the time, I had been a parent at the school for 13 years. During this time, I served on the SGB for three terms between 2006 and 2014. During my first term, I was the only 'coloured' parent on the SGB. During this time, I learned that while the children of teaching staff were exempted from paying school fees, children of administrative and cleaning staff were not, and hence did not attend the school. I also learned that the widespread and historical preferences afforded to alumni and siblings meant that there was physically very little space to offer learners without any historical ties to the school. I learned about 'top-ups', a practice which allows the SGB to supplement the salary of the principal as well as teachers, based on their performance. Of course, this kind of practice would only be possible at schools with funds. I learned about a life-long contract with a school uniform provider. I learned about the re-employment of retired teachers into other positions so that the same kinds of people remain employed by the school. A number of these practices were eventually dismantled – not without resistance.

I recognised throughout my tenure that the school had a long way to go in ensuring an inclusive space not only for diverse learner identities, but for a teaching staff, who had pretty much remained racially homogenous, despite shifts in learner demographics, albeit at a slow pace. As an SGB member, I became attuned to the internal power dynamics, both within the school, within the SGB, as well as the significant pull of its parent body. Nothing, however, could have prepared me for the events of 2017 to 2018.

Who chooses?

As my eldest daughter began to attend pre-school, it seemed a foregone conclusion that she would not attend the same kind of schools my husband or I had attended. South Africa's democracy meant that I could choose any school I wanted for my daughter – unrestricted by race or ethnicity. Schools, after all, were desegregated and as the slogan went, 'open for all'. Schooling for her would not only mean a curriculum cognisant of diverse communities and directed towards cultivating democratic citizens. It would also present the kinds of opportunities I hardly knew existed during my own school days: swimming and diving pools, tennis courts, hockey fields, netball courts, music centre, library and an IT laboratory. More importantly, in learning with children from diverse identities and backgrounds, she would, hopefully, acquire the respect and knowledge of how to engage with difference, what it means to live and become a confident member of a pluralist society. Did I doubt that I was doing the right thing in wanting a different schooling and educational experience for my daughter? Did it occur to me that I was sending her or her two siblings into environments not quite made for them? Could I have imagined that eight years after first sending my eldest daughter to a historically 'white' school, her younger sister would witness the same school turn into a battleground among parents, teachers, the principal, the SGB and the Western Cape Education Department (WCED)?

As already mentioned in Chapter 3, the migration of learners from historically disadvantaged ('black', 'coloured' and 'Indian') schools is driven by a desire for 'quality education', which is seemingly associated with better schooling resources and infrastructure, access to an array of sporting facilities and codes, smaller classes, more opportunities, as well as safer school environments. Allow me to immediately clarify a number of misconceptions which might arise from the phrase 'school choice' in South Africa (and I suspect elsewhere). While 'school choice' implies a choosing of schools by parents or learners, this is certainly not the case for the majority of parents.

First, while some parents get to choose, most do not. For 'white' parents and learners, gaining access into their first choice of schooling is a lot more streamlined than for those, who are not 'white'. The parents are alumni, some serve on alumni committees, or live in the residential area of the school. Or just being 'white' helps. Unlike 'white' parents, 'black', 'coloured', 'Indian' parents are not alumni (they were prohibited from attending 'white' schools);

they do not necessarily live in the residential areas of 'white' schools (racially-based residential clustering remains one of the hallmarks of apartheid). In sum, according to Woolman and Fleisch (2006), the majority of parents and learners cannot exercise choice relative to the products offered in the South African market because the costs associated with entrance into the market are prohibitively high:

> On the demand side, deeply entrenched features of the South African landscape – poverty, geographic isolation, limited housing stock, high levels of structural unemployment, the cost of travelling the enormous distance between home and school – conspire to lock the majority of South African learners out of the market. On the supply side, other deeply entrenched features – poor school infrastructure, the absence of multiple schools in many locations – effectively means that the product variation necessary for a market to form does not exist. (Woolman & Fleisch, 2006: 33)

Schools in South Africa are allocated into a quintile system, based on a pro-poor funding model. Historically disadvantaged schools receive more state funding than those which were historically advantaged. Schools allocated to quintiles four and five are deemed to be wealthier than those in quintiles one to three, with schools in quintile one and two, and many in three, declared as no-fee schools. While well-intentioned, the quintile system is fraught with contradictions, specifically with regard to the allocation of several historically disadvantaged schools to quintiles four or five alongside historically advantaged schools. Except for schools declared as no-fee schools, the SA Schools Act allows the SGB of all other schools to determine the school fees. One of the implications of a pro-poor model is that schools in quintiles four and five receive less state-funding and rely on school fees to supplement state funding. School fees are determined by the SGB. While most SGBs approach this mandate with an awareness of the socio-economic conditions of parents, a number of SGBs set exorbitant fees, beyond the reach of most parents, thereby creating renewed structures of exclusion. The point is, that when it comes to 'school choice', among a significant number of historically 'white' schools, it is the school that does the choosing, not parents and learners.

Given this commanding role, who is the school? South African schools rely on a decentralised model of school-based management, comprising the principal, the School Management Team (SMT) and the School Governing Body (SGB). In terms of section 23(9) of the South African Schools Act (DoE, 1996), schools are required to conduct SGB elections every three years. Beyond national, provincial and local government elections, the election of SGBs is considered among the biggest and most representative of community stakeholders in the country. As policy, these elections represent an example of democracy in action, as individuals from an array of backgrounds are invited to actively participate in the daily functioning of their child's school. The Schools Act stipulates that parents must constitute the majority of the members of the SGB. The sheer volume of responsibilities delegated to the SGB confirms their immense power. In setting the scene for the school's ethos and daily functioning, the SGB is responsible for designing all the policies. These include admission, language, religion, homework, discipline and extra-mural programmes; maintaining school property; recommending the appointment of staff; and managing the finances, which includes setting school fees (DoE, 1996), as well as any additional policies the school might deem necessary.

A careful reading of this list should immediately alert readers to the implicit knowledge and skills required by parents to serve on the SGB – skills which the majority of South Africa's parents and communities do not have, bringing into disrepute the capacity of parents to fulfil the mandate of school governance. These barriers notwithstanding, SGB's hold very powerful positions in schools, and in historically 'white' schools they can adopt practices, directed at the deliberate exclusion of learners from historically marginalised communities. They are also able to control teacher appointments –

whether appointed by the WCED or SGB. One of the main attractions of historically advantaged schools is their low learner-to-teacher ratio. A substantial portion of school fees is spent on employing additional teachers, not paid for the by the WCED. This attraction, however, is often used in the justification of high fees.

The tide turns...

By the time I concluded my last term on the SGB in 2014, I was still the only 'coloured' parent representative. Although the SGB diversified somewhat in the next election, the same 'white' parents were re-elected. During this time there were certain murmurs about increasing tensions on the SGB, but nothing was known for sure – not until the resignation of three members in August 2017. All three of these parents were part of the Inclusivity and Managing Diversity Sub-Committee of the SGB. One, a 'white' parent, also served on the Human Resources Sub-Committee and Transformation Sub-Committee. Not much was known about the reasons for the resignation, despite the three parents indicating that they had issued the principal and the SGB chairperson with a formal letter, noting their concerns. Various parents wrote to the SGB chairperson and principal, requesting that the formal letter of resignation be shared with parents, given that these parents had been elected by the broader parent body. The request was not accommodated, with the SGB chairperson issuing a vague statement on the matter. The poor handling of the matter resulted in a few parents meeting to discuss not only the SGB, but the overall strategy of the school in relation to diversity and transformation. The parent group became known as Parents for Change (PfC). By this time the three parents, who had resigned, had made their letter available to PfC. Below is an extract from their formal communication to the principal and SGB:

> From the beginning of our terms, we need to note that we were never treated as allies in the battle for inclusivity but

rather as adversaries impinging on someone's turf. The Principal in particular created an environment in committee meetings where it was tense and participants were fearful of speaking their minds ... We [the parents] have been told repeatedly that the school is on a journey to inclusion. We see the policies we have written shoved back in our faces in an attempt to prove that there is commitment. We have watched up close as to how this works and our opinion after 2½ years is that this is a tick box exercise without any real attempt to get to the very essence of the matter. One of the clearest ways of looking at this is to ask whether the learner feels like they operate in 'two worlds'. Do they feel like they have to behave in one way at home and an entirely another way at school because their school reality does not recognise and celebrate their norms and lived experiences? This is a vital part of the inclusivity and managing diversity paradigm.[4]

Requests for the SGB to distribute the letter to the school community, were refused. The PfC as well as other parents interpreted the principal and SGB's refusal to share the letter as a lack of transparency and accountability. It was therefore decided that PfC would disseminate the letter via its own parent networks. There were mixed responses. While some parents welcomed our action of sharing the letter from the three parents, others were unhappy with what they perceived as PfC 'trying to create problems'. To clarify our concerns, we managed to arrange a meeting with all parents, including the principal, senior staff members and SGB members. The meeting was facilitated by an external expert (arranged by the SGB), but even her expertise could not ward off the shameful racism encountered on the evening of 20 September 2017.

As the line between parents who wanted the school to transform and those who did not became firmly etched, there were vicious

---

4   Permission has been granted for the inclusion of these excerpts.

exchanges from and between parents. The evening culminated with a parent insisting on standing at the front of the hall to speak, rather than at her seat. She started with what I misread as a hopeful contribution. She shared her experiences as a Jewish parent who had always been subjected to being in the minority, and its subsequent discrimination. But then her story changed with a bold declaration that when 'black' children and teachers enter a school the standards drop. No doubt, she was articulating the thoughts of a number of parents and staff members in the room. But her bombshell was yet to come: 'If blacks don't like it at the school, they should fuck off!' What amazed me was not so much the brazen cheering of some parents, but the silence of the principal, who seemed to be lost in her role as the leader of this school community. Frantic efforts by the facilitator could do little to undo the damage of the parent's vitriol. The meeting had not gone as planned at all – I don't think any of us realised just how polarised we were as a parent community, despite the polite nods across playgrounds and netball courts. The only good to arise from the meeting was an even deeper resolve to change the school, at least by the increasing number of parents who decided to join PfC.

'Parents for Change'

When we first got together as a group of parents, it was with some unfamiliarity with each other. We might have passed each other in the corridors of school events or sporting matches, but very few of us of had ever had a serious conversation about how transformation was unfolding at our daughters' school. We were brought together by a common outrage, and more importantly, a determination to ensure that the school changed and functioned in harmony with a diverse society. Our first hastily arranged meetings took place at each other's homes or offices, often late into the evening. We came to these meetings from different histories and contexts.

When we formalised the group under the name 'Parents for Change' (PfC), there were 24 of us, pretty much representative of the diversity of the school in terms of race, culture, ethnicity, religion and language. As a collective we recognised and acknowledged that we are living in a society that is steeped in racism both overtly and subtly in terms of direct interactions but also, more specifically, systems and structures that are geared towards some people succeeding more than others. We also recognised that we had a responsibility in assisting the school in creating an environment where all learners and their families feel welcome, representative of the broader community and embraces the ideals of inclusivity and diversity. We endeavoured to realise our vision:

- By creating an open and collective space for parents, who wish to create schools, where all children feel a sense of belonging.
- By mobilising our voices and resources to bring about the change that will equip our children to evolve into responsible, responsive and compassionate human beings.
- By cultivating schools where all children learn how to engage with and respect difference.

Our emergence as a formalised group elicited a range of responses. There were parents who tried to dismiss our concerns as non-issues. There were others who accused PfC of wanting to sabotage their children's schooling, of sowing fear and animosity, and creating a climate of mistrust. Conversations with me ranged from odd to insulting. A 'white' mother, with whom I had been exchanging small talk for about five years shared that it was not true that certain parents did not want change, but that there should not 'be too much change'. My follow-up question on what she meant by 'too much change' ended both the conversation and whatever relationship we might have had.

There were two others that were especially disconcerting. One was with a 'black' father, someone with whom I had exchanged many conversations over the years, given that our daughters were in the same grade. He asked me why I was doing what I was doing – specifically, why I was creating problems for myself by trying to tackle racism when I should know that the school would never change. What about my daughter, he asked? Did I think about how teachers might victimise her because of me? His questions were not easy to dismiss. Was this about me, my own unfinished anger and frustration with the legacies of apartheid? In grappling with his questions, I asked him about his own position of non-involvement. He said that he was not only tired of fighting, but tired of being expected to fight. He just wanted to get on with living, to give his daughter the kind of life he could not have. In that moment, I did not have all the answers to his questions of me. But I thought about Yancy's (2005: 216) depiction of the hermeneutics of the body: how it is 'seen', its 'truth' is partly the result of a profound historical, ideological construction. 'The body', he explains, is positioned by historical practices and discourses; 'it is codified as this or that in terms of meanings that are sanctioned, scripted and constituted through processes of negotiation that are embedded within and serve various ideological interests that are grounded within further power-laden social processes' (Yancy, 2005: 216).

The other encounter was with a very agitated 'coloured' mother. She explained how she had struggled to get her daughter enrolled at the school, that she was 'grateful' that her daughter could attend, and the school 'was just amazing'. I listened intently as she praised the principal and all the teachers, concluding with: 'I send my daughter here because I want her to be taught by white teachers. If I wanted her to be taught by coloured or black teachers, I would have sent her to a coloured school'. She seemed to be unaware of the internalisation of her own oppression. She failed to see the extent to which she had succumbed to an 'inculcation of the racist stereotypes, values, images and ideologies perpetuated by the White dominant society about one's racial group, leading to feelings of self-doubt, disgust and disrespect for one's race and/or oneself' (Pyke, 2010: 553). This is the success of the colonial project – as 'a system of naturalising differences in such a way that the hierarchies that justify domination, oppression, and so on are a product of the inferiority of certain people and not the cause of their inferiority' (Sian, 2014: 68).

Shortly after the gut-wrenching meeting with parents, we sent a letter (dated 19 October 2017) to the Head of Education (HoE) at the WCED, the body responsible for all public schools located within the Western Cape province. In addition to our primary concern regarding the lack of transformation and inclusivity at the school, we highlighted the following:

- Resistance by the principal to any discussions and debates regarding inclusivity and diversity management, and a clear lack of commitment to any real change.
- The censorship of a teacher survey by the principal and SGB chairperson, when the level of fear, unhappiness and mistrust by teachers became apparent.
- The use of confidentiality agreements for SGB and SMT members prior to the commencement of every meeting, which feeds into a climate of suspicion and fear at the school.
- The wholly inadequate employment of teachers and administrative staff from a cross-section of South African society.

In 2017, of the full-time teaching staff, there were 31 'white'; six 'coloured' and one 'black' teacher employed to teach isiXhosa. Administrative staff comprised of seven 'white' and one 'coloured' employee; support (cleaning staff) consisted of five 'black' and seven 'coloured' members. The breakdown of the learner demographics was as follows: 68% 'white'; 19% 'coloured'; 9% 'black' and 2% 'Indian'. The letter was followed by a meeting (11 December 2017) between the PfC and three representatives of the WCED, including the provincial Head of Education (HoE). The meeting concluded with an undertaking that the concerns raised by the PfC would be investigated, and that separate meetings would be arranged with the SGB, the principal and staff. Thereafter, the WCED would arrange a facilitated meeting involving all parties, including the PfC.

By March 2018 there were several new developments at the school, which seemingly indicated more deterioration around issues of leadership, management and governance. A few teachers, who had been in support of transforming the school, had resigned. The SGB elections had seen the re-election of the SGB chairperson into the same position, and the election of only one 'black' parent. Contrary to the regulations of office bearers on the SGB, which stipulate that these should be occupied by parents (see SA Schools Act, no. 84 of 1996), the school's business manager, who is also responsible for the finance department, was elected to the position of treasurer. Most significantly, the principal had announced that she would be taking early retirement, effective at the end of 2018.

Despite letters from the PfC seeking a follow-up from the WCED (as promised in December 2017), it was only on the evening of 11 September 2018, that the HoE and representatives from the WCED would finally meet with the principal, and representatives from the SMT, SGB and PfC. Irrespective of different perspectives on what constitutes tangible transformational progress at the school, the meeting was reasonably positive, especially considering the SGB chairperson's renewed commitment to transparent communication and prioritisation of transformation. The deputy principal used the meeting to highlight a historical occasion at the school – the appointment of its 'first black African' class teacher (Anele)[5] in its 125-year history. As we parted ways on amicable terms, we were unaware of the dramatic turn of events the next day would bring.

On 12 September 2018, it became apparent that Anele had in fact 'resigned' during the day of 11 September 2018. Present at the meeting of her 'resignation' was the principal, the deputy principal and the SGB chairperson. This means that when the deputy principal made the proud announcement about the appointment of the school's

---

5   Not her real name.

'first black African', at least three people in the meeting with the WCED and PfC already knew about Anele's 'resignation'. Questions sent by PfC to the principal and SGB chairperson were met with the response that they were not at liberty to discuss the private matters of teachers in meetings. But then why announce her appointment in the first place? A subsequent letter (17 September 2018), bringing the matter to the attention of the HoE, was also met with a non-response. The disgraceful events surrounding Anele's 'resignation' would signal a turning point for PfC – not only in its already strained relationship with the principal and the SGB chairperson, but in what would become its (mis)placed trust in the WCED.

Anele[6]

While it is possible to draw parallels between Anele's marginalising experiences and my own at Erica High, there are significant differences, which is reason for greater concern. Anele represented a new generation of 'black' youth; she was born into South Africa's democracy and would not have had direct experiences of an apartheid political system. Most significantly, she also represented a minority of 'black' youth who had exclusively attended historically 'white' schools, followed by tertiary studies at the University of Cape Town. The additional fact that she had completed a learnership at the school for a year meant that she would have been initiated into the ethos of the school. It also meant that the school recognised enough potential in her to offer her the learnership in the first place.

It soon became apparent, however, via the circulation of WhatsApp messages among a group of grade five parents, that a number of parents were unhappy about having their children taught by her and questioned her suitability to the ethos of the school. In fact, as would be revealed later, at the very first parents' meeting with Anele, one of the parents asked to see her qualifications. The escalation of

---

6   Anele has given permission to share her story.

complaints was accompanied by parents insisting that their children be moved to other ('white') teachers' classes. Some even went as far as opting to home-school their children instead. Importantly, her 'suitability' had little to do with her competence or dedication as a teacher; her 'suitability' mattered only in terms of her race. 'Whiteness', explains Ahmed (2004), is represented as invisible, or unmarked, 'as a non-colour, the absent presence or hidden referent, against which all other colours are measured as forms of deviance'. Seeing whiteness, she continues, 'is about living its effects, as effects that allow white bodies to extend into spaces that have already taken their shape, spaces in which black bodies stand out, stand apart, unless they pass, which means passing through space by passing as white' (Ahmed, 2004).

'Black bodies', or people like Anele, 'confront whiteness in their everyday lives, not as an abstract concept, but in the form of embodied whites who engage in racist practices that negatively affect their lives' (Yancy, 2012: 7). This kind of scrutiny and maligned treatment are common for 'black', 'coloured' and 'Indian' teachers in historically 'white' schools. A language of 'standards' is often used as an alternative to more explicit mechanisms and expressions of racial or ethnic discrimination. Often, these standards are vague and exist in some kind of normative realm of how teaching ought to unfold, and more importantly, *who* ought to be teaching (Davids, 2019a). Being 'not-white' implies an absence of knowledge, skills, competence, and hence, value.

The principal and SGB (Anele was in an SGB post) responded by subjecting Anele to a series of 'mentoring' strategies, thereby bringing into disrepute her pedagogic authority in the class. This involved the submission of weekly and daily lesson plans, as well as assessment practices, to her head of department, and daily classroom visits at any given time by various members of the School Management Team (SMT). Against this backdrop, the widely reported question by one of her grade 5 learners, shared in the media: 'Are black teachers real teachers?' (Pather, 2018a), seems less surprising.

Despite Anele's complaints that she felt undermined and uninformed as to the objectives of the 'mentoring' process, the principal and SGB persisted in their course of action. The situation at the school created deep anxiety for Anele, and she began to feel increasingly alienated from her colleagues. It was at this stage that a parent wrote a letter (23 August 2018) to the principal and the SGB, raising concerns about certain parents' treatment of Anele. The SGB acknowledged the letter but never responded to the issues raised by the parent and seemingly failed to act on them. Anele would later share that she was given the option of 'resigning or face disciplinary action' which, according to the principal, would ruin her reputation. Not knowing how to respond, feeling insecure and without any support, Anele agreed to 'resign.'

Members from PfC met with Anele. She was assisted in lodging a grievance with the Commission for Conciliation, Mediation and Arbitration (CCMA).[7] The school defended its decision to ask for her 'resignation', citing, that parents had threatened to remove their children from the school. They could not, however, provide any written proof of providing her with details of the complaints, of issuing her warnings, or of the content and purpose of the 'mentorship programme'. After the initial CCMA hearing the school made her an offer that she could return as a learnership teacher. She refused and demanded compensation for the way she had been treated. The CCMA found that the school had indeed acted in a discriminatory fashion, that she had, in fact, been constructively terminated, and should receive an apology and compensation.

The finding by the CCMA of 'constructive dismissal' corroborated Anele's experiences of discrimination and humiliation. But as she pointed out, the apology from the school did not acknowledge the truth of what had actually happened. As confirmed by Anele, in the absence of support from a number of parents, it is doubtful that

---

7   The Commission for Conciliation, Mediation and Arbitration (CCMA) is a dispute resolution body established in terms of the Labour Relations Act, no. 66 of 1995 (LRA). It is an independent body, does not belong to and is not controlled by any political party, trade union or business.

she would have taken the route of approaching the CCMA. It is exceptionally difficult for teachers who experience discrimination or racism to act against these entrenched practices – not only because of their fear of reprisals, but because these practices are often deceptively disguised in a discourse of 'competence', which is used to systematically break down the self-esteem of teachers (Davids & Waghid, 2015). In most cases, professionals trapped in these kinds of scenarios recognise that their continued employment or possible promotion relies on their silence, and keeping their heads down.

Thank God for 'outrage manufacturers'

Anele's story did not end with the CCMA finding or the school's subsequent apology. The matter was widely reported in the media, setting into motion a series of events. On 6 November 2018, PfC held a press conference (see Isaacs, 2018; Fokazi, 2018). Although not specifically invited, the event was attended by an array of parents as well as teachers who wished to either share school experiences, or wished to forge ties with PfC so that our initiatives are extended into other schools. We had deliberately arranged to have the press conference at St. Mark's Anglican church, built in 1867. The church is located in District 6, an area originally established as a community of freed slaves, merchants, artisans, labourers and immigrants, with close links to the city and the port. Its iconic history of forced removals started with the 'resettlement' of the 'black' community in 1901. In 1966, District 6 was declared a 'whites-only area' under the Group Areas Act of 1950. Over 60 000 residents were forcibly removed to the Cape Flats, a desolate area, devoid of amenities and without transport links to the city centre, the hub of employment. The area of District 6 was systematically razed to the ground. It continues to be a haunting reminder of apartheid's brutality. It seemed apt, therefore, to host the press conference on a site of trauma and memory, to remind us of how little progress we had made since 1994.

The press conference had a series of dramatic effects. Almost immediately, several former learners from the school posted all manner of discriminatory experiences. Alumni shared how they were forced to 'become white' to have any sense of recognition and inclusion at the school (*News24*, 2018). These posts on social media had a ripple effect on past as well as current learners at other schools who also shared experiences of racist bullying, marginalisation and humiliation either by teachers, or learners. Up to this point, despite promises of addressing the concerns at the school, and despite the CCMA finding that the school had indeed acted in a discriminatory fashion against Anele, we had not received communication from the WCED. It was surprising, therefore, to read a statement issued by the Western Cape provincial minister of education in a newspaper. In it she states that 'a top public school in the suburbs of Cape Town' had acted appropriately in asking a grade 5 teacher to resign after 'ongoing legitimate concerns that were raised with her.' According to the minister, the apology issued by the school's SGB[8] was *not* for racism. Rather, stated the minister, 'The admission of wrongdoing by the school at the CCMA was because of issues of procedure regarding the process followed – SGBs are not experts in HR [human resource] processes' (Pather, 2018b).

Although the minister's statement reflected an intimate knowledge of the events and reasons leading to Anele's 'resignation', she continues that the WCED did not know about the allegations of racism in Anele's case. In justification of this ignorance, the minister claimed, 'The educator was employed by the SGB and not the WCED. The department, therefore, was not aware of the process relating to the teacher's appointment and subsequent resignation'. Quite paradoxically, while the minister made confident pronouncements that Anele had not been subjected to any ill-treatment, she seemed to be less informed about Anele's appointment or 'resignation'.

---

8   The apology reads as follows: 'the school unreservedly apologises to Anele* for the manner in which her employment was terminated and the circumstances surrounding such termination … As an SGB we have recognised that the school's institutional culture does not fully reflect the diversity of South Africa and we have publicly committed to changing this. It is a priority.'

Furthermore, there were additional arising questions regarding her commentary on the expertise of the SGB, her complete omission of any mention of the principal, and her rather odd claim that 'The SGB has informed me that they are working on a parent code of conduct which it has committed to make available to parents for comment' (Pather, 2018b). In our response to the minister (4 November 2018), the PfC noted the following:

- That the HoE had indeed been informed via letters and meetings about the concerns about racism and discrimination at the school, as well as the matter regarding Anele.
- At a meeting with the WCED on 18 September 2018, the HoE described the problems at the school as a 'governance' issue, thereby exonerating the WCED of any responsibility, and effectively ending all communication with PfC.

Two weeks after the minister's statement to the media, the then premier of the Western Cape (2009–2019), Helen Zille, offered her views on a Facebook post on 17 November 2018. Like the minister, she claimed to have 'inside knowledge' of the school, and presumably the treatment of Anele. She ignored the underlying issues regarding poor transformation at the school. Instead, she referred to PfC as 'outrage manufacturers', waging 'orchestrated attacks' on the school, intent upon getting 'as much political capital out of the situation as possible.' Zille is correct in using the term 'outrage' to describe PfC. We were outraged by a simmering anti-transformation culture. These included a systematic decline in learner enrolments from historically marginalised groups; a principal and SGB chairperson stone-walling any initiatives directed towards transformation and inclusion on the basis of not having funds for these initiatives (yet, during this same period R4 million had been allocated to a shared hockey astroturf and R7.5 million to a pool upgrade); censorship of a teacher survey because some teachers were courageous enough to express their experiences of a school environment mired in fear and mistrust; the use of confidentiality agreements for SGB and SMT members prior to the commencement of every meeting as a means of shutting down any dissenting views. Moreover, we were as outraged by the systematic 'constructive dismissal' of Anele as we were by a provincial education department that showed no inclination towards ensuring schools are spaces free from racism, discrimination and harm.

On the surface, it might seem odd that a school-based incident would attract inputs from both the minister and premier. And yet, it is not odd at all – not if one understands the extent to which schools and education are used as political tools in maintaining the status quo and preserving the privilege of a few. Schools are not autonomous or neutral zones. Schools are prone to furthering their own interests, and facilitating subtle mechanisms that reproduce social inequality, despite the scholastic narrative of equal opportunities for all (Masschelein & Simons, 2013). To try to understand the problems related to governance at advantaged schools as one pertaining to the exclusion of significant parent-stakeholders (Carrim, 2001), is to reduce these problems to ones of external representation, and to misrecognise the deep entrenchment of 'whiteness' in our schools and societies. Outrage is exactly what is needed 'to *disarticulate* whiteness from those juridico-political, economic, institutional, aesthetic and other locations that will resist disarticulation to ensure the maintenance of white power' (Yancy, 2008: 238). The 'white' body is implicated in and productive of racialised spaces; it is tied to the operations of the state as a powerful site of 'white' hegemony (Yancy, 2008). To him, deploying critical pedagogies in the name of valorising cultural heterogeneity in schools as a strategy for disrupting whiteness as normative is one thing. Contesting and undoing the racialised material structures and discursive orders of 'white' imperialism is another (Yancy, 2008).

The ensuing mismatch that arises from an under-representation of diversity among teachers has consequences for both dominant and minority groups. It is not simply a matter of ensuring space that is reflective of a broader society. It has to do with schools fulfilling an ethical responsibility in relation to all learners, and hence, all learning. On the one hand, numerous studies confirm that minority-group learners benefit from the 'insider knowledge' of minority group teachers. On the other hand, both minority and dominant groups stand to benefit from a diverse teaching corps in terms of witnessing the qualities and capabilities of people, regardless of race, ethnicity, culture or sexuality (Achinstein et al., 2010; Kohli & Pizarro, 2016; Ingersoll et al., 2019). There are myths that we each have of each other. We employ these myths in how we come into the presence of others. Sometimes with openness and hospitality, other times with scepticism and hostility. Schools have a powerful role to play in unlearning these myths. They should therefore be held to a higher standard not only in what they teach the children in their care and the kinds of spaces they cultivate, but in what they fail to do. Creating an inclusive space where children are free from prejudice involves a sensitivity to who teachers are, and what they stand to bring. Safeguarding the value of all teachers, and indeed, all their values, is critical to the responsibility of education to democracy.

As highlighted in this chapter, parents can be as much of a negative influence as a positive one when it comes to the education of their children. Schools are abundantly versed in the management of different parent personalities, whether in the form of over-zealous involvement in school projects, or abusive rantings from spectator stands. Parents on governing bodies should be treated with the same level of detachment. That their positions on SGBs look like they are fulfilling a democratic imperative of school governance, does not mean that they are interested in democratisation of schools or education. In the same vein, the historical departures of colonialism and apartheid do not infer that these two ideologies are no-more. There are other ways, explains Santos in conversation with Sian (2014), through which occupation continues – not foreign occupation, tutelage and the prohibition of a state formation, but other forms of occupation.

Domination exists in the relationship between the coloniser and the colonised, which is why the powerful grip of internalised oppression cannot be discounted. Domination, as Santos (Sian 2014) reminds us, never acts in pure forms but in constellations of oppression. Schools and SGBs, for example, do not explicitly use race as a criterion for inclusion. Instead, they use constellations of oppression, such as school fees, residential proximity, language with regard to learners and a language of standards and competence with regard to teachers. To counter these narratives, we need a postcolonialist discourse of subversion and interruption, a non-acceptance of singular truths and the perpetual entrenchment of binaries which seek always to establish a line between 'us' and 'them'. For this reason, to *be* in a postcolonialist space is to be attuned to the unending processes necessary for the disruption of 'othering' and oppression.

5

Lost in diversity

The fundamental objective of apartheid (literal translation, 'apartness' or separation) was to maintain and ensure 'white' supremacy through the implementation of separation along racially-constructed lines, which was formally institutionalised in the apartheid laws of 1948. The Population Registration Act 30 of 1950, explains Erasmus (2017), legislated the recording of each person's race in South Africa as one of the following: 'white', 'native' and 'coloured', with 'Indian' as a subcategory of 'coloured'. According to Erasmus (2017), under Section 1 of the Registration Act 30 of 1950, the classification of 'white' was defined as 'a person who in appearance obviously is, or who is generally accepted as a 'white' person, but does not include a person who, although in appearance obviously a 'white' person, is generally accepted as a coloured person'. The classification of 'native' referred to a 'person who in fact is or is generally accepted as a member of any aboriginal race or tribe of Africa'. The ruling National Party, which propagated apartheid, began to use a classification of 'Bantu' instead of 'native' (Erasmus, 2017). By 1978 the racial descriptor of 'Bantu' was replaced with the racial classification of 'black'. In turn, the Population Registration Act categorised 'coloureds' as neither 'black' nor 'white', positioning 'coloured' as an intermediate category between essentialist constructs of 'white' and 'black'. To Erasmus (2001: 13), this kind of social engineering encouraged 'coloureds' to believe that they were 'not only not white, but less than white; not only not black but better than black'.

South Africa's democratic narrative, while wrapped in words and colours of diversity, continues to rely on apartheid-constructed racial categories, which belie its moral intent of equality and social justice. Attempts at re-signifying the categories 'black', 'white', 'coloured' and 'Indian' in terms of a transformational tracking, and hence a transformative initiative, suggests not only an inability to break from a race-based past, but presents a palpable barrier to an anti-racist society. There are implications for this retention – most of which we can theorise about, but my fear is that, in holding onto that which divided us in the first place, we might not know how to come or be together. I centre this chapter on what I describe as a bruising collision with this misinformed transformation – one which I should have seen coming (theoretically), but knocked me, nevertheless.

Trapped in the shadows

How do I belong as a woman, who, depending on geopolitical contexts, is neither 'black', nor 'white'? My home country, despite its rhetoric of democratic pluralism, underscored by an ideology of non-racialism, continues to rely on and employ the very racial categorisations deployed during apartheid – oddly justified under the auspices of tracking transformation. Every time I complete any government forms, banking applications, or claims for external work undertaken at other universities, I am compelled to select either a 'B' (for black), or 'C' (for coloured), or 'W' (for white), or 'I' (for Indian).[9] My efforts to ignore these are often returned as 'incomplete' forms. Other efforts to select the 'B' are at times 'corrected' by government officials, the moment they see me or my identification document photograph.

As officially defined by the South African government between 1950 to 1991, the term 'coloured' (formerly 'Cape Coloured') represents a person of mixed European ('white') and African ('black') or Asian ancestry. Individuals assigned to this classification originated primarily from 18th- and 19th-century unions between 'white' men and slave women or between slave men and Khoekhoe or San women. The slaves were from Madagascar, the Malayan archipelago, Sri Lanka and India.

Distinctive about the term 'coloured' in a South African context, it its specialist denotation to people of mixed racial ancestry, rather than one who is 'black', as it is more commonly understood in other contexts (Adhikari, 2013). Other common features that have historically marked 'coloured' communities, explains Adhikari (2013), include a strong association with Western culture and values in opposition to African equivalents, their claim to an intermediate position. Consequently, not only am I foisted with a racial categorisation, which seemingly does not exist outside of South Africa's borders, but my own 'non-racial' government has gone to great lengths to explain to me, and all others like me, that we are definitely not 'African Black'.[10]

In one sense, states Adhikari (2013), 'coloured identity is a product of European racist ideology which, through its binary logic, cast people deemed to be of mixed racial origin as a distinct, stigmatised social stratum between the dominant white minority and the African

---

9   University forms generally include explanations such as: 'For the purposes of conducting an analysis on the workforce profile, and to ascertain which of the existing contractors are from designated groups in terms of the Employment Equity Act'.

10 In South Africa, the category of 'black' is used in two ways: one in a generic sense when applied as in the case of Black Economic Empowerment (BEE), and the other when used in specific reference to a population group, 'African Black' or 'Black African'.

majority.' In its objective to classify and control people, the colonial state played an important role in demarcating social identities by imposing racially based legal categories and segregatory policies on the population. In another sense, however, 'coloured' identity is also very much the product of its bearers who, according to Adhikari (2013), were in the first instance primarily responsible for articulating the identity and subsequently determining its form and content.

Regardless of the uncertain and contested nature, the 'coloured' population was vital to the apartheid project and was used as a social and spatial buffer between essentialised 'white' and 'black' populations in social and spatial engineering projects (Hammett, 2010). Perceptions of 'coloureds' as both relatively privileged and disadvantaged – less than 'white', but better than 'black' (Erasmus, 2001) – created tensions between post-apartheid state attempts to reify this population category, individuals' self-reification of colouredness, and individuals' erasure and rejection of racial identifiers (Hammett, 2001). It was hoped that the transition to democracy would result in a shift to nonracialism. This, however, explains Hammett (2001), has not been realised, not only because the government has failed to provide a coherent strategy for dealing with race in a post-apartheid milieu, but because race and ethnicity are being reinscribed as central to debates about citizenship, rights, diversity and claims to marginalisation in the new socio-political context (see Adhikari, 2004; Battersby, 2005). Hence, we see that despite an emergence of a vocal, 'coloured rejectionist' voice within the non-racial democratic movement of the 1980s, 'the past decade and a half has witnessed a resurgence of Colouredism with many people who had rejected the identity reembracing it' (Adhikari, 2004: 168). Adhikari (2004) maintains that fear of African majority rule, perceptions that 'coloureds' were being marginalised, a desire to counter pervasive negative stereotyping of 'coloured' people, and attempts at capitalising on the newly democratic environment in pursuit of political agendas have all played a role in fuelling 'coloured' assertiveness in the new South Africa.

It has become commonplace, says Adhikari (2004) for 'coloured' people disaffected with the new South Africa to express their disgruntlement by lamenting that 'first we were not white enough and now we are not black enough'. Besides accentuating their interstitial position within a transforming South African racial hierarchy, it captures their perennial predicament of marginality (Adhikari, 2004). In addition to the profound reform measures promulgated by a transition to a democracy, it is important to pay attention to how racial identities are continually shifting and reconstructing. As recognised by postcolonial theory, racial signifiers and identities are fluid and contextual and work beyond the inadequacies of the static and fixed nature of modernist identity categories (Hammett, 2001). As such, contends Hammett (2001: 250), we must take account of the 'contextual framing of identities and the continually shifting ways in which ideology, lived experience, and negotiations of external expectations are layered into the continual remaking of identities.'

Inside and out

I live in a province known as the Western Cape.[11] At the time of writing, of South Africa's nine provinces, the Western Cape is the only one not under the dominant political leadership of the ANC. It is governed by the Democratic Alliance (DA).[12] This means that while the rest of South Africa falls within the ambit of the governing party of the African National Congress (ANC), the Western Cape is subjected to a provincial government, which considers itself in opposition to the national government. It is worth providing some insight into the political influences the DA comprises. On the one hand, the DA has as its party predecessors the Democratic Party (DP), established in

---

11 South Africa has nine provinces: Eastern Cape, Free State, Gauteng, KwaZulu-Natal, Limpopo, Mpumalanga, Northern Cape, North West and Western Cape.

12 South Africa is a constitutional democracy with a three-tier system of government and an independent judiciary. The national, provincial and local levels of government all have legislative and executive authority in their own spheres. This means although a province is governed by the ANC, a municipality can be DA controlled.

1989 when the Progressive Federal Party (PFP) merged with smaller liberal parties – the National Democratic Movement (NDM) and the Independent Party (IP). Describing its roots as being in 'liberal South African politics', the DP opposed apartheid and supported full voting and other civil rights for South Africa's 'black' majority and constitutional changes toward that end. On the other hand, in 2000 (six years after South Africa became a democracy), the DP formed an alliance with the New National Party (NNP) and the lesser known, Federal Alliance (FA) to form the Democratic Alliance. In joining forces with the NNP, it essentially aligned itself with the former National Party – the same party which (mis)ruled South Africa by propagating apartheid and 'white' supremacy from 1948 to 1994. Hence, while the DA might be correct in its assertion of holding historical anti-apartheid roots, its post-apartheid alliance confirms a 'white' supremacist influence.

This, then, is my socio-politico-economic home – a country governed by the ANC, which prioritises the economic empowerment of 'blacks' over that of 'coloureds' and 'Indians', and a province, governed by the DA, which, after a limited dabbling with 'black' leadership, has re-emerged as a 'party for whites, led by whites' (Southall, 2020), despite having a significant 'black' membership. The political, social and economic restoration which underscored the Grand Narrative of the Struggle against apartheid, is seemingly devoid of ethical restoration. Had ethics entered or influenced the Grand Narrative, I would not be writing this chapter. Instead, the retention of apartheid-based categories not only extends an ongoing racially divisive chronicle by turning South African citizens against each other, but prevents them (us) from seeing others as human beings, from reaching out to each other.

My enforced construction as a 'coloured' woman has disposed me to liminal and limitless spaces of 'othering', uncontained by the assemblages of 'white' and 'black'. These spaces spill over and adopt unfamiliar and unexpected formations as I visit across geopolitical borders. Those unaware of the terminology of 'coloured' express confusion, even offence, when I attempt to explain my South African assigned label. While South Africa's democracy has undoubtedly released me from the ideological prerogative of apartheid and has afforded me social and economic access and mobility, I remain trapped in the afflictions of identity-based politics.

Recently, I applied for the position of dean of the Faculty of Education at the university where I am based. I did so with confidence. My academic record was certainly exemplary enough to attract numerous accolades from my university. I had a professional record confirming years of immense experience in my primary discipline of education, collaborations with national and provincial education departments, interactions and relationships with key role-players in the education sector, as well as ties with colleagues at a range of international universities. At the time of applying, I was the head of my department. By all accounts, I had every reason to believe in the success of my application. I was encouraged by colleagues both within and outside of the university. To my understanding, the application process followed a standard route. An interview committee, consisting of members from the Faculty of Education (academic and administrative), as well as representation from other faculties, human resources, the senate and the university council. I might be omitting one or two other representatives. Normally, the committee for the appointment of executive positions is chaired by the university vice-chancellor and rector, but in this case, it was chaired by the Deputy Vice-Chancellor: Social Impact, Transformation and Personnel. I am uncertain why this was the case, but it did not present a deviation in terms of policy.

I cannot be sure how many applicants applied for the position. I do, however, know that five or six of the applicants were invited to be interviewed by the interview committee. My interview must have been well-received, given the news that I was one of two final candidates. Three steps remained: presentation to and voting by the faculty; voting by the senate; and a final decision by the University Council. After the presentations by the candidates, each was subjected to a series of questions from faculty members, after which the faculty was required to vote on their preferred candidate. This process was overseen by the chairperson of the interview committee. As per protocol, neither of the two candidates was present during the voting. The penultimate step in the process involved the university senate – the highest academic body of the university.[13] The CVs of both candidates were made available to the senate. During this session it was made known that I had secured the highest votes from both the faculty and the senate. I had every reason to feel very confident about my prospects. But then matters took a horrible turn.

While unexpected, I would be dishonest if I said I was entirely surprised. I had had enough historical experiences in professional (mis)interactions, whether applying for a position, or for funding for a project, that applications are not considered along a straight line of overtly stated criteria and requirements. Things are never what they seem, even when you think there is trust in the room. There are certain games that necessarily have to be played, certain hoops that require jumping through, certain people's ears in which whispers are required. There are those who are on the inside, and those who are not. I honestly do not know why I thought this particular application would be any different. I can only explain it in terms of confidently believing that my academic record was good enough to meet the demands of the position. I had irrationally thought that the appointment would be based on merit, and as an extra, my obvious commitment to the institution. Little did I realise, how I ashamed I would become of my own naivety.

A phone call from the rector informed me that I was not the

---

13 The Senate comprises the rector and vice-chancellor; the rector's management team; the registrar; two members of University Council; professors of the university; five associate professors; four members of the Students' Council; two members elected from their number by the permanent academic staff of the university who are not professors or associate professors; two members elected from their number by the administrative staff of the university; two members elected from their number by the technical staff of the university; departmental heads who are not full professors; and such additional persons as may, by resolution of the senate, approved by the council, be declared to be members of the senate.

successful candidate. The university had instead opted to appoint an 'African black' candidate from outside the university. The decision, I was told, was made by University Council, who seemingly discounted the votes from both the faculty and the senate – a move, I was told, that was, in fact, their prerogative, but which, of course, begs the question: Why bother with attaining these two sets of votes in the first place? The news coincided with a more painful unfolding circumstance in my life – literally, on the same day, two hours apart – a diagnosis of terminal cancer for my mother. In hindsight, her illness buffered me against what I was experiencing professionally. Faced with the death of another parent, it was easy enough to shrug off the disappointment of not having been appointed. Events and perspectives have a way of placing people and life into priority.

That would have been the end of the matter – disappointment, after all, is a natural part of lived experiences, holding the capacity to either motivate or demotivate us.

Except, for the two phone calls from two different people that preceded the one from the rector – one, two days before council convened to decide on the appointment, and the other on the morning of the council meeting advising me to withdraw my application. The decision had already been made – it would not be me. The voices on the other end of these two phone calls were very confident in their advice to me. I had no reason to doubt either of them. Yet, I did, thinking and hoping that surely the council would not go against the vote of the faculty and the senate.

I try not to think about these two phone calls too much. The mere thought is demoralising and saps too much energy from me, takes me down too many well-trodden paths of previous encounters with discrimination, marginalisation and exclusion, and leaves me feeling rudderless. I remain uncertain about how to account for what happened in this case. A follow-up meeting with the rector did not shed any light, other than to offer me a somewhat empty and questionable reassurance of the value I bring to the institution. My own thoughts wander across intersectional possibilities of exclusion.

Is the appointment of an 'African black' to be interpreted as more progressive than that of a 'coloured' female? Or are my experiences in South Africa's democracy a mere extension of my experiences in South Africa's apartheid? Am I to accept that my liminal position as a 'coloured' precludes me from a transformational discourse defined along an uninterrupted continuum between 'white' and 'black'? Or is there another layer of 'othering' at play – a layer which sits not only in my religious identity, but in the expression of that identity in my hijab? Is there a place for people, who look like me in post-apartheid South Africa? And then flowing from the latter question – how do I begin to make sense of this? Do I turn to South Africa's historical normative legacy of 'white' Christianity, or do I search for answers in the ever-increasing regulation, victimisation of Muslim women in other liberal democracies? It is virtually impossible to expect any answers to these complex questions. Institutions are seldom known for their integrity, only for their *management* thereof. They *do* diversity even when they have worrying distorted understandings of what diversity holds and implies.

Some months after the events described above, I found myself listening to a presentation by a recruitment agency, employed by my university. The presenter proudly shared the success, thus far, in recruiting and appointing 'black' candidates at the university. His treatment of diversity as a racial audit (seemingly the only portal of historical reparation), revealed a seriously deficient understanding of the pervasive and intersectional nature of inequalities. As far as the presenter was concerned, as long as the university proceeded with its current employment rate of 'black' academics and administrators, it was well on its way to transformation. I suppose it would be unfair to expect anything beyond the function of a recruitment agency, which is to recruit the kinds of individuals described to them by the university. More worrying, is not only that the strategy employed by the university seems less concerned with challenging inequalities, but that its recruitment strategy functions as a technology of concealment, where inequality is hidden by the very measurements of 'good' performance (Ahmed & Swan, 2006). As such, diversity and equality become forms of capital within organisations which circulate through the distribution of documents and 'good feelings' (Ahmed & Swan, 2006: 98). The entire meeting pivoted around racially-based statistical progress, without any consideration of the implications for identity expressions. There appeared to be no sense of the depth and intricacies of apartheid's oppression. And there is evidently no compass in terms of historical restoration and justice. In this regard, diversity is a term used to show change without being bothered to reflect on what that change should mean in relation to equal and unbiased recognition.

Whether or not my race as a 'coloured' played a role in my non-appointment remains mere speculation. I can certainly not dismiss my other identity markers as a woman, or as Muslim woman, or as a hijab-wearing Muslim woman – categories, which while intersected, attract and warrant very different kinds of attention. It is impossible to ignore the normative institutional identity and culture of my university, which is 'White, male, Afrikaans, Christian, heterosexual and able-bodied' (Le Grange, 2021). I fall short in four of these markers, placing into perspective the out-of-placeness of both my personal and professional identities. In this regard, intersectionality takes stock of the 'converging and conterminous ways in which the differentiated and variable organising logics of race, class and gender and other social divisions such as sexuality, age, disability, ethnicity, culture, religion and belief structure the material conditions which produce economic, social and political inequality in women's real lived lives' (Mirza, 2013: 6).

It is obvious that post-apartheid South Africa needs redress; this redress necessitates a reversal of the kinds of policies that ensured the political, social, economic disenfranchisement of *all* people who were not 'white'. First, however, a reversal of policies cannot mean turning the same policies onto another group – that is, by simply restructuring historical hegemonies. Second, attempts to re-frame apartheid's mandate and oppression as limited to a 'white'/'black' dichotomy are misleading and duplicitous, because they reduce or ignore the oppression and displacement experienced by those categorised as 'coloured' or 'Indian'. Revealing an indifference to the complex vectors of other potential exclusionary factors, such as gender, religion, language, culture, ethnicity, sexuality and class. This indifference, asserts Lugones (2016), found both at the level of everyday living and at the level of theorising of both oppression and liberation, is insidious. She explains that 'it places tremendous barriers in the path of the struggles of women of colour for our own freedom, integrity and wellbeing and in the path of the correlative struggles towards communal integrity' (Lugones, 2016: 13).

I am reminded of the somewhat effervescent debate between 'Black Lives Matter' and 'All Lives Matter', and specifically, Judith Butler's response in an interview with George Yancy (Yancy & Butler, 2015). She explains that when some people proclaim, 'All Lives Matter', their message is not untrue, but they misunderstand the problem. It is true, states Butler, that all lives matter, 'but it is equally true that not all lives are understood to matter which is precisely why it is most important to name the lives that have not mattered, and are struggling to matter in the way they deserve' (Yancy & Butler, 2015: 6). To concretise the universal formulation, 'All Lives Matter', one that truly extends to all people, continues Butler, 'we have to foreground those lives that are not mattering now, to mark that exclusion, and militate against it' (Yancy & Butler, 2015: 6). There are many lives in South Africa, and no doubt everywhere else in the world, that do not matter – whether on the basis of race, culture, ethnicity, class, caste, religion, gender, disability or sexuality.

In emphatically foregrounding the economic privileging of 'blacks' in South Africa, the government's actions are no different to that of the apartheid state – that is, the premise of racial privileging remains intact. And so, yet again, my body as a 'coloured' woman is subjected to the same nodes of discrimination, only this time under the guise of a democracy. It is hard to shrug off the sense of betrayal, not only of a history of political struggle against racism, but of a present in which human beings can still not come together without their skin colour pre-determining how they are to be seen and treated. How are we expected to breach the schisms engineered during and through apartheid, if we hold on to systemic structures of racial profiling and discrimination? More importantly, on what do I base my sense of belonging when I live in a province and state that subjects me to a tug-of-war between 'white' and 'black' privileging? During apartheid, I had a much clearer sense of non-belonging as an oppressed citizen; it was unequivocally clear. I was prohibited from living in certain areas; attending certain schools; working in certain positions; having fun on certain beaches, or at certain swimming pools; standing in certain queues at the post office, hospital, or police station; travelling in certain sections of the train or bus; watching a movie in certain cinemas; or just sitting on certain park benches. It was a life of immense regimentation and regulation, so frustratingly controlling and disheartening, which is why any sort of discrimination in a purportedly democratic society is so infuriatingly contemptuous.

Diverse but not equal

The very spaces in which I find myself – the agora, my university – simultaneously invite me in, while still holding me at bay. That universality of equality remains restricted by the setting in which it is expected to operate (Mohanty & Tandon, 2006), implies not only that those institutions do not exist in isolation, but that 'what you actually are obliged to look at is more and more framing' (Spivak & Grosz, 1990: 5). As such, institutional experiences within the university have to be explored by taking account of the broader centre-periphery construction outside of the university. More specifically, as Spivak et al. (1990: 40–41) observe, 'there is nothing that is central. The centre is always constituted in terms of its own marginality ... in terms of the hegemonic historical narrative, certain peoples have always been asked to cathect the margins so others can be defined as central.' We saw this during apartheid, and we see it now during democracy.

South Africa's path to a 'citizenship of equality' has been absorbed into a problematised language of 'diversity', which seemingly approaches the term as an indicator of difference, without accounting for the differences within that difference. While intent on promoting diversity as a hallmark of South Africa's new-found democracy, it falters in recognising that, despite widespread policy reform in terms of a creating a racially just society, these reform measures have not adequately confronted the deeply systemic and structural racism of an apartheid society. It is meaningless to compile policy after policy onto a foundation which was never constructed on ethical values in the first place. Consider the following two excerpts. The first is from the Department of Higher Education and Training (DHET, 2019: 6):

> The Employer [DHET] fully embraces the provisions of the EE Act and affirms its commitment to government's socio-economic transformation policy. Employment Equity initiatives interlink and require complementary processes to be active and in place in the DHET, such as Change Management, effective management of diversity in the workplace and an Organisational Culture mind shift to accommodate previously disadvantaged groups namely black people, women and people with disabilities.

The second one is from Stellenbosch University (SU, 2021) (my institution), entitled 'Welcome to Employment Equity & Promotion of Diversity':

> Employment Equity is not only a legal compliance requirement, but also one of the strategies to accelerate transformation as articulated in SU vision 2040 and Strategic Framework 2019–2024. The University strategic theme of 'Employer of Choice' clearly articulates the following goals:

- Embraces diversity and equity, leverages unique talents and strengths, promotes life-long learning and celebrates achievements.
- Creating and promoting an enabling, inclusive, equitable, healthy and safe working and learning environment that encourages our diverse staff to maximise their productivity, and where they feel valued and contribute to SU's excellence.
- Talent acquisition and talent management plan, which includes equitable remuneration.

While a desirable organisational characteristic, diversity could be achieved by changing human resource practices, rather than something connected with tackling structural inequalities in society (Deem & Morley, 2006). The language of the two policies above is in line with liberal paradigms, wanting to project a transformative and positive public image. To Ahmed (2006), documents do not simply have a referential or descriptive function; they do not simply describe principles that a university already has. Rather, Ahmed (2006: 114) elaborates, 'by producing the university as if it was a subject with such principles, the documents then become usable as they allow practitioners to make members of the university as well as the university itself as an imagined entity subject to those principles.' She goes on to say that this kind of image-creation or rebranding, allows the university not only to conceal racism, but it also works to reimagine the university as being antiracist based on its claim of embracing diversity. Statements of commitment, or policies, might do something 'because they enable the exposure of a gap between what organisations say they do, and what they actually do: indeed, they might "do something" insofar as they fail to describe what organisations do' (Ahmed, 2006: 114). Following Ahmed (2006), it is easy to see the politics of diversity as an institutional performance, but which becomes an obstacle to both diversity and equality. Diversity is judged in terms of what the document states, rather than what the university *does*.

In the context of policies on widening participation in higher education and the media exposition, explains Mirza (2006: 101), 'diversity' has become an 'all-consuming discourse that no right-minded university, old or new, would dare be without as an intrinsic part of its identity and image.' The dilemma of exclusively associating diversity with equality, is that it not only discounts the centrality of other kinds of vocabulary, specifically, 'anti-racism' and 'social justice', but it individuates difference, conceals inequalities and neutralises histories of antagonism and struggle (Ahmed & Swan, 2006: 96). My own experiences hint that I am paradoxically invisible in my visibility. Here, I am not referring to women who are aware of gender bias in the workplace and use 'intentional invisibility' to limit their exposure to it. In opting for a risk-averse, conflict-avoidant strategy, they consciously draw less attention to themselves, portray themselves as nice by being less assertive, and avoiding conflict with colleagues (Fielding-Singh et al., 2018).

What I am referring to is that my appointment as a 'coloured' woman at a historically 'white' institution renders me visible, a visibility which undoubtedly, is enhanced by the fact that I am a hijab-wearing Muslim woman. However, this distinction in my difference can also reduce me to invisibility, in the discounting of my voice and participation. That is, I am perceived as so different, so removed and beyond the realm of familiarity and comfortability of the structural functioning and ethos of my university, that a consideration of voice and agency is implausible. I am not necessarily seen as bringing any value to my institutional space – suggesting that my experiences of struggle and antagonism are as pertinent now, as they were historically. Conceptually, and in practice, diversity is seldom all encompassing or all-accepting; there are limitations to what diversity can hold – limitations which are always enclosed by who holds the lens or perspective. In this way, a recognition and foregrounding of diversity can, in fact, have a paradoxical effect of extended, if not deeper, marginalisation.

Depending on the context, the paradox of diversity becomes evident in different ways. One dominant manifestation resides in the proverbial glass ceiling, typically encountered by women as they hit mid-management. In the academe, state Alcalde and Subramaniam (2020), women are not simply denied top leadership opportunities at the culmination of a long career, but rather such opportunities seem to disappear at various points along their trajectories. Globally, and generally, membership statistics of women in the academe do not correlate with leadership positions. Stated differently, while universities might be inclined to employ women as faculty members, they are less inclined to appoint the same women as leaders in the university. In South Africa, despite significant strides being made in the representation of women from historically marginalised groups, the occupations of senior positions in the academy, reveal a different picture – there is a glaring gap between being a member of the academy, and being a leader or manager thereof.

At the time of writing, South Africa's 26 universities are occupied by four female vice-chancellors. More worrying is the report from Universities South Africa (USAf), that since 2015 there have been 20 vacancies for vice-chancellors, but only four of these positions have been filled by women. Closer to home, only one woman serves on the executive management team of my university, while four women occupy positions as deans across ten faculties – all of whom are 'white'. One of the implicit drawbacks of this kind of gender imparity, is that the minimal or solo appointments of women into leadership positions, place them at greater scrutiny, and hence, visibility, typically not framed in positive evaluations (Alcalde & Subramaniam, 2020).

When it comes to women from minority groups, the glass ceiling is lowered. American 'women of colour' are underrepresented in tenured and full professorships, which in turn limits opportunities to advance into formal leadership positions at colleges and universities (Alcalde & Subramaniam, 2020). While the language of diversity is often defended because of its inclusiveness, its neglect in terms of naming specific social categories, such as race, gender, class, ethnicity, sexuality, means that it can negate the specific experiences of these categories. Collectively, states Jones (2006) 'black' and ethnic minority women academics have not attained the progressive benefits that have accrued to 'white' women in the wake of gender equality initiatives and directives; by focusing on gender as a generic category, the slower progression of 'black' and ethnic minority women academics is obscured. In South Africa, the situation is hardly any different, and when it comes to 'coloured' women, this obscurity is enhanced because of their misrecognition as not being 'black'.

Since the event described in this chapter, I have spent many moments reflecting on my function and role at my university. The experience that I have been subjected to as a 'coloured' body is certainly not anomalous. It is deeply situated in countless accounts of similar forms of 'othering', neither erased, nor lifted by South Africa's path to a democracy. The past, it seems, continues to find its presence in the now. There are certain changes in me – some bad, some good. I have hardened to my own citizenship, recognising that my desire for an equal chance and equal footing will not be realised in my lifetime. This pains me, at times. Other times, it leaves me ambivalent – knowing that I could not know and feel what I do, that I could not write what you read here, without living the life that I do. And, I suppose, that's the good – a recognition, that our experiences can force us into a consciousness we ordinarily might not have had. It's not just my writing that has changed, it's also my teaching. I am more focused on what my presence might bring, on my silences as much as my speech, and who I turn towards. The relegation to an insider-outsider status creates ambivalence about my own liminality, but it also allows a vantage point I might not have had.

6

(Dis)embodied intersectionality

The theological centrality of Muslim women resides in the foundational source codes of Islam – that is, the Qur'an, as God's revealed text, and the Sunnah (example of Prophet Muhammad PBUH). As a 7th century revelation, and in response to a deeply patriarchal society, the Qur'an brought about far-reaching changes in relation to gender reform as regards marriage, divorce and inheritance (Esposito & DeLong-Bas, 2001). Like participants in other faiths, Muslim women are socialised into deeply embedded practices and traditions, which at times demonstrate commonalities, and, other times, distinguish them from other faiths. Within these practices are added layers and nuances as different interpretations yield different ways of being and acting – influenced and shaped by equally embedded cultural and contextual norms. How Muslim women dress and practice Islam is always influenced by the cultural milieu in which they are located (Davids, 2020a). As an illustration of the contestation surrounding Muslim women, particularly in liberal societies, Cooke et al (2008:

91) have constructed the neologism 'Muslimwoman' to illustrate how the veil, real or imagined, functions like race, a marker of essential difference, which Muslim women seemingly cannot escape.

The concern for Cooke et al. (2008) was to find a way to draw attention to the post-9/11 collapse of religion and gender into a singular and imposed political category. She wished to highlight the ways in which non-Muslims and Muslim religious extremists alike deploy this newly entwined religious and gendered identification that overlays national, ethnic, cultural, historical and even philosophical diversity in order to control Muslim women. 'Muslimwoman', explain Cooke et al. (2008: 91), draws attention to the emergence of a new, singular religious and gendered identification that overlays national, ethnic, cultural, historical and even philosophical diversity. Underscoring these re-configured and intersected identifications are conceptions and interpretations of cosmopolitanism, which according to Cooke et al. (2008: 92), are 'at once unifying and diverse because the more people identify with and connect to each other, the more their identities will be hybrid and split among the multiple groups in which they act and want to belong'.

Implicit, therefore, in the theorising of intersectionality is that my experiences of the world, or rather, the world's experiences of me, are not singular. Who I am, or what I embody, cannot be isolated or sequestered to disconnected nodes of identity. I am at once layered, complex in my multiplicities of being – female, 'coloured' and Muslim. The value of intersectionality is that it recognises that all identities and group identities do not enter and participate in the public sphere as equals. Some enter as individuals and are seen as such. Others, however, do not. And when they do not, the way they are seen and interpreted is never as an individual. That they are not seen as individuals is symptomatic of the accompanying presumptions, seldom couched in unbiased fairness. While the usefulness of intersectionality resides in its capacity to systematically expose the multiple structures of potential marginalisation and exclusion, it also confirms the multiple points of vulnerability and resistance which have to be mediated by a body like mine. This mediation is not new. The profound 'othering' of Muslim women is as prominent in colonialist discourse as it is now. I have witnessed this 'othering' as subject and observer with both intellectual astonishment and emotional disgust. I am drenched into a marker of 'Muslimwoman', inscribed by stigmas of backward passivity – a living paradox, reduced to what I choose to wear, which, although symbolic of sexually constrained, fundamentalist domestication, seemingly equally capable of inflicting global terrorism.

'Othered' into humiliation

As had become my routine, after leaving work, I would pop into my local supermarket, about one minute from my home. The routine included a regular parking bay, a nod at the 'parking attendant', and an always warm greeting from the security guard, stationed at the entrance to the shop. I must have seen and greeted him a thousand times over – sometimes he would walk me to my car, patiently waiting for my trolley as I unloaded goods into my car, happy to delight me with stories of his day. Interacting with him was as much a part of my shopping experience as deciding what groceries to purchase. But then things changed. Things between the security guard and I, things between the world and me. It is funny when I phrase it in this way, it sounds almost ridiculous, but that is the way I remember it – the day I became aware of how the way he saw me had altered, or is it, in the way I was altered to be seen by him?

The afternoon had unfolded in a predictable way: I had left work and picked up my one-year-old son from my mother, who had been baby-sitting him. He had been fussing in the car, continuing as I unbuckled him from the car seat. My hands and arms were filled with my handbag, my son, car keys and his toy car. In my distracted rush into the entrance of the supermarket, I remembered to greet the security guard. But his face was not there to respond. Instead, he stepped towards me, without a smile, and instructed me to open my bag. I was confused, taken aback by the absence of a smile on his face, and his no eye contact. Had I done something? Had something happened to him? I could not understand what he was asking of me. My confusion quickly swirled as I realised that as he was waiting for me to open my bag, other shoppers were passing me by, uninterrupted by a similar instruction. I asked him why. He mumbled about following orders from management, still no eye contact. As I insisted on knowing why, he became more uncomfortable, finally meeting my gaze with a set of pleading eyes to not make his job difficult. What was his job, I wondered? What had changed over the past two days?

Even as I pushed the only answer from my thoughts, I knew there could be no other. It was the day after 9/11. I turned away, headed towards my car, face flushed, my body filled with anger, humiliation, vows never to return to a very conveniently located and stocked supermarket. It took me a while to settle down, to process my feelings, to understand what had transpired on an otherwise nondescript afternoon. What had changed between the security guard and me? Nothing, except the world around us. He had been instructed to no longer see me as just a shopper. The request to search my bag was a message that I represented a potential threat, in need of surveillance and scrutiny – a procedure not without degradation. For me, the interaction with the security guard would signal the beginning of a new narrative, one in which my hijab would have a starring role, both locally and internationally. Intersectional 'othering', as Mirza (2013: 7) details, arises at unique historical moments – that is 'when the category "Muslim woman" is invested with a particular affective and linguistic meaning', and is (re)organised into systematic social relations and practices.

Typically, we conceive of humiliation as demonstrative of the power of one person over another; the capacity to humiliate another is often framed in hierarchical relationships of power – as in teachers and learners, a parent and child, an employer and worker. But humiliation can also manifest in ways outside of these frames, as in the case of a security guard and a shopper, where the presumption or adage that the customer is always right is trumped when the shopper is deemed to act in a devious way (such as stealing an item), or in my case, deemed to present a threat by virtue of my dress code. The humiliation emanates from an emotional experience of an unjust action. In being singled out and asked to open my bag, I suffered an injustice. I left the shop, feeling wronged, unsure of how I could return my body as a Muslim woman to the site of my humiliation.

I know that the horror of 9/11 is not the source of the suspicion and antagonism my hijab evidently attracts. I know that my narrative slots into a long-standing historical preoccupation with the veil (hijab), its orientalist allure, its symbolic entrapment with oppression, sexual repression and backwardness, its incongruency with the West, and since 9/11, its heightened provocation of suspicion, hostility and fear. Often described as 'the day that changed everything' (Morgan, 2009), 9/11 signalled my entry into a world much more comfortable in its disdain of Islam and its followers. My encounter with the security guard on 12 September 2001 would become an unwelcome, repetitive template in my life. Airports are the obvious sites of my greatest discomfort – with my visit through Warsaw Chopin airport deserving a special mention.

In full view of other travellers, I was ordered to stretch out my arms for a search, which included an over-zealous ground-staff member, shoving her hands beneath my hijab, urgently feeling for whatever explosives, while simultaneously reassuring me that this disgraceful intrusion onto my body was 'merely routine'. In situations, like these, I have learnt that there is no room for resistance or questions. I have learnt that, the softer my compliance, the greater the likelihood of the imposition coming to an end. My husband, who had been travelling with me, was waiting on the other side, his face a contortion of disgust and pity at witnessing my disgraceful violation. It is hard writing about this moment, not because I cannot recall every uninvited touch up and down my body, but because I am returned to a time of powerlessness, a victimisation, captured in a capsule over which I have no control. I could only co-operate, staring ahead, as the rest of the airport went about its business around me – with none of its occupants being too distracted at witnessing a security guard running her hands under my hijab. I can confirm that there was nothing 'routine' about my humiliation, or about my presence on the streets of Warsaw while attending the 15th Annual International Network of Philosophers Education (INPE) conference at the university of Warsaw in 2016 – serendipitously entitled, 'Philosophy as Translation and the Understanding of Other Cultures'.

My most recent clash with airport officials occurred on 21 March 2021. The date is important as it signals the celebration of Human Rights Day in South Africa – an irony certainly not lost in the events I am about to share. Upon walking through the 'control' gates at OR Tambo airport in Johannesburg, South Africa, I was approached by a security guard, hands outstretched, wanting to 'feel' my head scarf. I was taken aback and refused to be touched by her for two reasons: she had no basis for wanting to 'feel' my headscarf, and Covid regulations demanded a 1.5 m social distance between us. She persisted, drawing the attention of an Airports Company South Africa (ACSA) employee, who informed me that it was 'protocol' to 'check all headgear'. The security guard informed me that if she could not 'feel' my hijab, I would have to remove it, so that she could see my hair. I refused. She explained that all hats needed to be removed. I pointed out that wearing a hat is not the same as wearing a hijab – the one is a clothing or fashion accessory, I wear my hijab as a religious obligation. I requested to speak to her manager. She arrived promptly and informed me that it was ACSA's policy and protocol to 'check all headgear', including braids and cornrows. She could not, however, provide me with a copy of the policy or protocol. I could also not find any mention of this on ACSA's website. After maintaining my refusal to co-operate, the manager explained that she could not see what was beneath my scarf, hence the need to check. I pointed out to her that she also could not see beneath my dress, yet she was not asking me to remove any other item of clothing. She replied that that would be a 'criminal offence'. Following her logic, it is a 'criminal offence' to ask someone to remove his/her dress or clothing, but it is not a 'criminal offence' to ask Muslim women to remove their scarves.

Realising my disbelief in her argument, the manager then went on to claim that there were 'many cases' in which women with dreadlocks and scarves had smuggled drugs through the airport. I assumed she was referring to the case of a South African, woman, Nolubabalo Nobanda, who smuggled 1.5kg of cocaine in her dreadlocks, through Suvarnabhumi Airport in Bangkok in 2011. I could not, however, recall any other cases. And I could neither recall, nor find any cases (when I conducted a subsequent online search), involving hijab-wearing Muslim women smuggling drugs, or any other kind of paraphernalia under their scarves. Throughout our exchange, we had a full view of the control gates through which I had just passed. During this time, at least three hijab-wearing Muslim women had passed through the gates – all of whom were subjected to a security guard 'feeling' their scarves, blatantly disregarding social distancing and not sanitising between the touching of the women. However, 'black' women with heavily braided hair-dos, as well as two wearing head scarves, passed through the gates without any interference. None of these women were stopped to have their braids or scarves checked. The manager witnessed this with me, and when I pointed out that it is clear that the 'protocol' is reserved for Muslim women, she replied that the officials should have stopped the other women.

Admittedly, I would not have adopted my combative position had this incident taken place at an airport outside of South Africa. While my confidence derived from being on home soil, the encounter left me feeling disappointed and humiliated. Disappointed to witness and experience that South Africa is following dominant trends in the profiling and criminalising of hijab-wearing Muslim women and humiliated in yet again being subjected to practices of discrimination and marginalisation. I wrote to ACSA the next day, complaining about the treatment to which I had been subjected and requested a copy of the policy dictating the 'searching of all headgear'. I received an automated response that provided me with a reference number and an assurance: 'We will attend to your query in the next Business Day'. At the time of writing (about seven months later), I had still not received any correspondence from ACSA. My complaint to the South African Human Rights Commission has still not yielded any action or intervention, nearly a year later, despite numerous assurances.

Other highlights include heavily paused delays at the gates of Heathrow, JF Kennedy, O'Hare and Rome–Fiumicino – involving very limited verbal exchanges, but a protracted examination of my passport and all other supporting documents for the apparent audacity of my visit. My birth country is no different, even when it involves inter-provincial flights – with ground-staff often at pains trying to explain why my identity document requires checking at the check-in counter, the baggage counter, and again just before I board the actual plane. These kinds of checks have become a normal part of any trip. It requires more emotional perseverance and gritted teeth than any congested long-haul flight. Muslim colleagues and friends advise me to simply remove my hijab and spare myself all the 'unnecessary drama and stress'. While I understand this advice, and have seriously considered it, I am not convinced that travelling or any other endeavour ought to involve a change in how I choose to enact my identity as a Muslim woman – not if doing so has nothing to do with my safety or the safety of others.

While slightly more manageable and without the threat of being turned away at airports, my encounters in other settings have not been any more forgiving. Except for two occasions, I have consistently found myself in professional environments in which I fall into a minority group category – both in terms of race and religion. And, might I add, even when women constitute the majority in terms of numbers, male dominance continues to hold sway. I have been questioned a number of times on why I wear a hijab. While some are genuinely interested in my response, others prefer to hold on to their own opinions, usually of the sort that I am probably forced to do so by a domineering spouse or my rigid faith. Even when my own version is accepted, there is a comeback of 'yes, but other Muslim women don't wear it'. I do not know why other Muslim women wear a hijab, or in fact, why they do not wear a hijab – such discussions seldom come up among my circles of friends or family, it is simply not an issue. I am always amused by how random strangers lay claim to understanding the dynamics and imperatives of group and individual identities. One of the things that comes to mind during these encounters is the familiarity that some assume in asking the question in the first place. I do not necessarily feel it is my business to ask others about their faiths, or how they choose to practise them. There seems to be a particular kind of objectification of Muslim women's bodies which allows for uninhibited practices of examination and scrutiny.

My presence at my university is not without some uneasiness. In addition to supervising postgraduate students, I teach two postgraduate programmes: philosophy of education to students registered for the Postgraduate Certificate in Education (PGCE), and BEd (Hons) educational leadership and management. For many of the PGCE students, of whom the majority are 'white', I represent their first encounter with a hijab-wearing Muslim academic. Most of them would probably have gone through their entire schooling career being taught by only 'white' teachers. Over the years I have witnessed a significant shift in how students respond to me. Most simply see me as their lecturer or supervisor. A few, however, struggle to reconcile the way I present with their image of a teacher – not only in terms of race, but also in terms of religion and culture. While some approach this struggle through questions and dialogues, others come to me enveloped in years of socialised resistance to anyone who is 'other' to them. While one student concluded his academic year with me by sending me a very lengthy email about his stereotypical views and 'hatred' of all Muslims – which thankfully shifted over the course of the year – another sent me a YouTube video on Muslims who were 'saved' by converting to Christianity. I have learnt to accept these kinds of responses and actions as part of my own educational moments.

Muslim women as paradox

What is it about the hijab that makes it so off-putting? Why does it elicit the kinds of responses or commentary that it does? It seems that for as long as I have written on this topic, the more urgent and troubling the questions have become. The liberal democratic landscape is flooded with regulations and prohibitions pertaining to the hijab in the public sector, prescribing not only how Muslim women ought to dress, but deliberately defining the hijab as an item irreconcilable with 'democratic' norms. Significantly, laws governing the prohibition of the hijab coincide with the Western 'War on Terror' narrative, which has ensured increasing discrimination against Muslim minority groups in the United States and Europe (Wing & Smith, 2006). Evidently, the 'War on Terror' extends onto certain bodies, irrespective of any political or 'terrorist links.' Ahmed (2003: 392) elaborates on the idea that particular signs are associated with particular bodies; anybody who looks Muslim or Arab 'could be terrorists', and hence, deserving of a 'war'. Interestingly, one of the most common questions directed at me, whenever I visit the United States, whether from taxi drivers or conference attendees, is whether I am Arab. My responses that I am in fact South African, are met with disbelief, and followed by repeat questions of where I am from 'originally'. Seemingly, my hijab reinscribes me onto another nationality – one which more easily aligns with a 'terrorist look' and 'war'. It is a troubling re-inscription in that it deliberately misrecognises me into a predetermined, homogenised box, not only in terms of geopolitical context, but in terms of somehow legitimising the stereotype that all Arabs are terrorists. The prospective narrative of a South African national presents a disturbance to the homogenisation of Muslims as an errant group of terrorists, and of Muslim women as being without agency.

Seemingly, at the heart of the desire of liberal democracies to de-veil Muslim women, is to not only 'liberate' them from the symbolic oppression of the hijab, but also to curb terrorism, and enhance the assimilation of the migrant population (Abdelgadir & Fouka, 2020). Binary constructions of hijab-wearing Muslim women as a priori oppressed are crucial to the narrative of the West as liberator. Consequently, while Muslim women are 'sexually constrained'; 'ignorant, poor, uneducated, tradition bound, religious, domesticated, family-orientated, victimised', Western women are constructed as 'educated, modern, as having control over their own bodies and sexualities, and the freedom to make their own decisions' (Mohanty, 1988: 65). To Hargreaves (2000: 53), the veil operates as a symbol of cultural difference; it represents the 'Otherness' of Islam and is 'condemned in the West as a constricting mode of dress, a form of social control, and a religious sanctioning of women's invisibility and subordinate socio-political status'. In sum, instead of regarding 'non-Western' customs as symbolic of cultural diversity, differences are reduced to a clash of values (Mancini, 2012), with the veil being (mis)used as a literal barrier that not only prevents the integration of the female Muslim body into Western society, but marks her for social and economic exclusion, stigmatisation and criminalisation (Petzen, 2012). Kirmani (2009) observes that the scholarly interest in Muslim women has its foundations in the orientalist fascination with the veil and the harem, which helped to construct a picture of Muslim women as symbols of the brutishness of colonised peoples and the symbolic 'other' to Europe's rational civilization. Fundamentally, the veil is constructed as a rejection of 'our way of life' (Khiabany & Williamson, 2008).

These interpretations are seemingly irreconcilable with Muslim women's actual motivations for wearing the hijab or veil. Reasons for wearing the veil include religious compliance, personal piety, family and societal pressure, symbols of identity or cultural or political assertion, and resistance to sexual oppression and objectification (Kirmani, 2009; Golnaraghi & Dye, 2016). Despite particular Qur'anic verses, which call upon Muslim women not to display their beauty, and to draw their veils (verse 24: 31; verse 33:59), there are various, often contesting, interpretations as to whether the veil is indeed an obligatory garment, or whether it should best be understood in terms of particular historical, sociological, or political contexts. To Hussain (1984) and Mernissi (1991), the Qur'an's reference to veiling can be understood as a metaphorical or physical barrier, it does not explicitly address women's clothing. Similarly, Ahmed (1992) argues that there is no direct Qur'anic exhortation that women should veil themselves; rather that the injunction pertains to the need for modesty on the part of both men and women. Other views, like those espoused by Al-Qaradawi (1982), hold that Muslim women are under obligation to cover their whole body, except their face and hands, when in the presence of strange men. In sum, there is as much disagreement on whether the veil is obligatory or not within the community, as there is among Muslim women's motivation for wearing it. What connects the varied views, however, is the idea of the veil as a manifestation of a particular kind of identity – whether as social, religious or political expression (Davids, 2020a).

In turn, experiences of Muslim women in liberal democracies stand in stark contrast to those of women in Indonesia (a Muslim-majority country), where veiling has been shown to increase as a result of the expansion of female participation in the formal sector that is shaped by the prevailing culture of gender relations and might therefore be a sign of economic modernisation (Shofia, 2020). Shofia (2020) asserts that unlike common depictions in liberal democracies, women who veil in Indonesia do not seem to signify low social status or lack of education. If anything, says Shofia (2020), the probability of donning the veil is significantly and positively predicted by education, suggesting that veiling might be a cultural strategy used by Muslim women in weathering gender-related social norms, which generally locate women in domestic roles and responsibilities. Similar trends were found among Muslim women in Egypt, who opted to wear the veil because it opened socio-economic opportunities (Mahmood, 2005).

Notably, in singling out Muslim women for scrutiny and (re)dress, liberal democracies fall into the same domain of which patriarchal

Islam stands accused – namely, that Muslim women are without autonomy and agency, and are compelled to succumb to patriarchal norms, which include veiling. Stated differently, if Muslim women are presumably wearing their hijabs because they are forced to do so by a patriarchal religion, then how should one describe the actions of liberal democracies, when they, too, force Muslim women to alter their dress code? Both positions and arguments construe Muslim women as without agency, without voice, and in need of being spoken for and acted on behalf of. More worrying is the unashamed mobilisation of integration through forceful assimilation, and states Mancini (2012: 411), 'cultural homogenisation which aims at anchoring European identity in secularised Christianity, while at the same time reinforcing the systemic nature of gender oppression'. Not only have private reasons for veiling become the content of public debates and law-making, but Muslim women occupy a deeply paradoxical space, cast simultaneously as victims of patriarchal oppression, and a threat to Western modernity. Being veiled, explains Mancini (2012), is likely to be perceived as a woman's refusal to engage in what are taken to be the 'normal' (Western) protocols of interaction with members of the opposite sex and thus, as a violation of the notions of gender hierarchies established within Western social structure.

Confronting the intolerance of liberal democracies

Murad (2020: 24) poses the question: 'If we must be intolerant of intolerance, then can liberalism tolerate anything other than itself?' Although the discourse of integration relies on claims of openness to others, there seems little to suggest that liberalism is interested in any other identity that does not resemble itself (Murad, 2020). Quite evidently, if one looks at the dominant trends pertaining to the treatment of Muslim women, the implicit expectation is that the 'other' needs to adopt the dominant ways of the West.

There are two pressing concerns arising from this perceived clash between Muslim women and liberal democracies. The first pertains to the construction of the hijab as irreconcilable with gender equality, as defined by Western feminism. This exceeds external manifestations of dress regulations. It speaks to an interference in how Muslim women live in their faith and how they choose to enact it. The template of a Western normative reflects the implied inherent universalism of Western feminism. Mohanty (1988) draws critical attention to the ways in which Western feminism has used universal categories to understand women's experiences and gender relations. These categories, however, are derived from their own experiential frameworks, not from women rendered to the category of 'third world', which of course includes Muslim women, and who are seen as objects, rather than subjects of knowledge.

Ahmed (1997: 30) explains that the 'third world woman' is 'interpreted in terms of a Western understanding of gender oppression: the representation of her as a victim of a universal patriarchy positions the Western feminist subject as an authority, while taking the West as a reference point for understanding different forms of power relations.' The way out of this dichotomous construction between 'Western' and 'third world' women, underscored by a politics of universal judgement, argue both Mohanty (1988) and Ahmed (1997), is a sensitive and contextualised approach to cultural specificity and difference, towards a politics where judgements are made possible only through specific engagement. It is only through engagement that one gets to understand the perspective of the other. This is not only a matter of unlearning the violence of universalism, maintains Ahmed (1997: 31); it is also about 'enabling a different kind of ethical relation between subjects (differently and unequally positioned by the international division of labour) which is based on a more mutual engagement'.

The second concern moves from a universalist understanding of 'third world' women, and relates to the presumption by liberal democracies that they have enough insights into the lived experiences of Muslim women that allows them to make decisions on their behalf, not only in terms of how they should dress, but how they should be and act. The intrusive actions of wanting to regulate the dress code of Muslim women assume a right to 'get inside the skin of the other' and close enough to 'the truth of the other's (well) Being', states Ahmed (1997: 32). There are inherent presumptions of intimate knowledge of the Muslim woman as object. Her presumed backwardness, oppression and subservience have been used by Western feminism in liberal democracies to think and act on her behalf. The Muslim woman cannot be presumed to have a voice or agency, since this would denounce her need for re-presentation. The construction of the Muslim woman as an-already-known object readily justifies the irrelevance of engagement with and knowledge *from* her. There is no need to speak to a Muslim woman, there is no need to understand why she does what she does, and why she wears what she does. There is only knowledge of the self, which is seemingly sufficient to disregard other kinds of selves and their knowledge.

By assuming that one already knows the other and their difference, explains Ahmed (1997), the self and other relations are held in place.

To Ahmed (1997: 32), 'Such a politics, whereby the Western feminist simply refuses engagement with the other, hence does not move the Western feminist into unlearning (beyond the unlearning of her right to speak), nor does it move the other from its position as always already the other'. It is immensely difficult, therefore, for Muslim women to break from a theoretical script, which continues to construct Muslim women as nothing else but a victim or a villain, an empty symbol of undesirable cultural 'otherness'. Of all the assigned signifiers, the one which is probably most critical to the Western theorisation is that of Muslim women as oppressed. What this signifier secures is a negation of agency. The negation of agency is painfully central to a scaffolding argument that unfolds like this: Muslim women are oppressed, and hence, do not have agency. Because they do not have agency, they cannot have the capacity to freely choose to wear the veil. Supporting the hijab, therefore, is akin to supporting oppression. More importantly, however, the negation of agency feeds into the theory, which not only designates Western feminism as the saviour of Muslim women as 'third world' women but appoints Western feminism as the agent of Muslim women.

Consequently, before I can even get to the point of (re)claiming my own agency, I have to disprove my oppression by proving that my own account is worth writing and telling. I have to show that normative accounts of who holds agency can and should be disrupted. I have to be careful in how I traverse this setting because, in addition to being a priori oppressed, any articulation from my side is paradoxically interpreted as resistant to Western norms, and hence, inflated to a threat. This is the unequal positioning of my identity as a Muslim woman, which continually forces me into 'knowing my place', being careful not to say too much, but also not to say too little, but forces me to say something if the unethical discourse which exists *about* me is to be disrupted. Hence, inasmuch as I have no desire to speak on behalf of other Muslim women, I also recognise the unequivocal importance of not only representation, but representation with voice. When I confront that which seeks to mark, box, marginalise, exclude and criminalise me, I do so with the weight of knowing that I am not alone in my experiences, and that it matters that I speak out – not only against those who position me as 'other' to them, but also against those who share my religious identity. This is a discussion I turn to in the next chapter.

7

Patriarchy as religion

It is not only in the public or professional sphere that I have experienced routine practices of 'othering' and prejudice. Although framed and expressed differently, I have had similar experiences within the community of my faith. Inasmuch as I struggle to find a sense and experience of equality within a South African society – whether social or professional – my position as a woman within a Muslim community is not without turbulence. While my collision with the public sphere intersects across markers of race, gender, religion and culture, my conflict with my Muslim community is entirely gender based. My seeming inability to establish a relationship of equilibrium can most clearly be explained as a schism between what I interpret Islam to embody and espouse, and what I witness some Muslim men *as doing*. I have come to understand that my internal inclusion is contingent on my willingness to accept and participate in normative practices of patriarchal subjugation. Speaking out or writing against that which I understand to be as contradictory to the paradigmatic sources of

Islam (the Qur'an and Sunnah), have, at times, provoked new (mis) markers, which I elaborate on in this chapter.

Since I can remember, I have always looked for representations and narratives of myself within my religion. Where are the women? Their voices? Their histories? Their experiences? Their contributions? My early encounters with *madrassah* teachers generally left me both dissatisfied and disinterested – not so much with what I was learning, but with what I was not being taught. Looking back, most of my boredom and disinterest stemmed from an over-emphasis on memorisation and rote learning, with minimal accommodation for conversation and deliberation, let alone interrogation. During my early teens I was fortunate to begin to encounter different kinds of teachers, who not only introduced me to a more dialogical relationship with my faith but affirmed the need for a curiosity about what I know and believe as a Muslim. This same curiosity is probably what led me to a doctoral study, focused on the lived experiences of Muslim women, their inclusion and belonging in a cosmopolitan society.

I have particular observances of what it means to be a Muslim woman in a Muslim community. I have observed notable discrepancies and contradictions between what I understand Islam to state and espouse, and what I have witnessed. And I have understood these disparities to stem from a substantive neglect of the historical and contemporary role of Muslim women, socially, economically, politically, and hence, epistemologically. Instead, and despite widespread gains being made by female Muslim scholars and women in (re)claiming their rightful place in Islam, the prevailing interpretations of what ought to constitute the role and treatment of Muslim women in my own community, remain framed in a predominance of patriarchal defence and preservation. Patriarchy, states hooks (2004), is a political-social system that insists that males are inherently dominating, superior to everything and endowed with the right to dominate and rule. The essence of patriarchy is supremacy of the father figure, and its rules are based on blind obedience and the repression of emotions and non-conformist thoughts (hooks, 2004). Although men derive greater benefits, patriarchy is as damaging to men as it is to women.

'Too big for her boots'

The mosque serves as a space for a shared expression of Islamic religiosity, communal identity, as well as social, intellectual and cultural services. It is considered as much as a sanctuary for individual introspection as it is a centre for educational programmes and congregational prayers. Certainly, when Muslims perform their obligatory pilgrimage (*hajj*), performing prayers and supplications in two of Islam's holiest mosques – *Masjid al-Haram* in Mecca and *al-Masjid an-Nabawi* in Medina – are obligatory. Despite its theological, social and cultural centrality, Muslim women do not always enjoy seamless access and participation in the mosque.

The works of various scholars and activists in different settings confirm mosques as being gendered spaces, regardless of whether they are in Muslim majority or minority contexts (Lewicki & O'Toole, 2017; Nyhagen, 2019; Ghafournia, 2020; Nas, 2021). Attempts by women to access and participate in mosques in a number of Muslim majority and Muslim minority countries are viewed as a physical intrusion or condemned as sacrilegious (Hoel, 2013; Nyhagen, 2019). Depending on mosque committees, which are almost exclusively dominated by men, women are forced to navigate degrees of exclusion: no provision of space at all; no provision of ablution facilities for women; peripheral or inadequate and unmarked spaces, often used for other activities, other than the sacred activities of prayer.

While there is a dyadic relationship between the absence of women in leadership positions and their exclusion from the mosque, both of these expose a gendered pulpit, and reflect dualistic ontological convictions steeped in gendered symbolic orders – that is, God as male (Hoel, 2013). Evident are severe practices of gender segregation, underscored by an androcentric and sexualised worldview which relies on excluding women as a means of retaining male hegemony.

The exclusion of Muslim women from a number of mosques around South Africa is a persistent feature, albeit less the case in the Western Cape. Either there are no physical spaces designated for women (mosques generally function along gender-segregated lines), or if there are, these are re-purposed *not* for the patronage of women. During the 1980s – at the height of the struggle against apartheid – the 'women in mosques' campaign gained some leverage in ensuring access and accommodation for women. The campaign provoked scathing rebukes from certain religious leaders, who viewed the inclusion of women as contrary to normative interpretations of Islam. Over forty years later, the same exclusionary practices persist. A group of Muslim women based in Durban and Johannesburg[14] were excluded from participating in the standard evening prayers (*tarawih*), which take place during the month of Ramadan.[15] In their complaint, the women described their exclusion not only as 'a culture of patriarchy and sexism in the mosques', but 'against the teachings of the Qur'an'; 'This culture is so entrenched in the community that it seems like it's Islamic law' (Masweneng, 2018). The treatment of the women, and their persistence in returning to the mosque, has given rise to the formation of a group, known as the 'Women of Waqf'.[16]

I was angered and disappointed, not only by the despicable treatment of the women by a few men, self-ordained as the custodians of mosques, but by the distorted message presented about Islam, and how it purportedly (dis)regards women. In response, I wrote a piece entitled, 'How Muslims betray Islam by not allowing women in the mosques' (Davids, 2018a), published in a national newspaper. I knew that the article would ruffle patriarchal feathers. In turning

---

14 South Africa has nine provinces. Durban is located in the province of KwaZulu-Natal, and Johannesburg is based in the province of Gauteng.
15 Ramadan is the ninth month of the Islamic lunar calendar in which fasting is prescribed for all Muslims. There are, however, exemptions for a number of categories of conditions, which include poor health, pregnancy and travelling.
16 *Waqf* is an inalienable charitable real estate endowment under Islamic law.

directly to Qur'anic verses (see, e.g., Chapter 4; Chapter 33, verse 35) in support of equality between men and women, I disrupted two hegemonies. One pertains to male-interpretive norms, which rely on female subjugation and marginalisation in order to retain their authority. And the other relates to a disruption of males as the sole interpreters of the Islamic faith.

The revelation of the Qur'an in 7th century Arabia saw the introduction of fundamental reforms of customary law. These include a woman's right to a contract marriage, to inherit, and control over her dowry and property. Her pervasive importance is made evident in the fact that there are more passages in the Qur'an that address issues pertaining to women, as individuals, as part of a family and, as members of a community, than all the other issues combined (Wadud, 2002). Furthermore, historical accounts place women as key participants in the propagation and dissemination of Islamic knowledge; they are described as freely studying with men and other women – both in study circles (*halaqāt*) and at the *madrassah* (Ahmed, 1992; Afsaruddin, 2005). Women constituted a 'normal presence at all times and on all occasions at the time of the Prophet' (Auda, 2017: 31). These accounts present a counter-narrative to the ones advanced by a male-interpretive privilege. In addition to the indisputability of history, there is the discursive emphasis on the importance of social justice, not only in the Qur'an, but in the practices of the Prophet Muhammad – rendering any kind of exclusion or discrimination readily out of sync with Islamic tenets.

My article was published on 7 June 2018. By the time I opened my laptop early that same morning, there were already a number of emails in my inbox, bearing the title of my article in the subject line. Most were in support of my sentiment. One respectfully asked me to withdraw the article, asserting that it portrayed Islam in a bad light; that I should instead engage directly with the *ulama* on these matters.[17] A reasonable request, and one which I have on

---

17 *Ulama* refers to the religious leaders or theologians in Islam; they are viewed as the interpreters and guardians of knowledge, including Islamic doctrine and law.

many occasions acted upon, including on this occasion. Like all other conversations on matters of controversy, there appears to be a breakdown between what the *ulama* say in private, and what they are prepared to pronounce on publicly. I could not, however, withdraw the article. First, because my article concerned the actions of a group of Muslim men, whose actions had misrepresented the teachings of Islam. In calling this out, I am not portraying Islam in a bad light, I am arguing that the exclusion of women from the mosque is bad. Second, silence on these matters, I believe, allows this kind of injustice to persist.

On the next day, I received another email with the subject line: 'women in mosques.' No salutation or signature; just a question: 'Are you Hanafi, Shaafi, Shia, Salafi or what?' My insider status as a Muslim told me that this was a question less for clarification than the basis for another kind of hostility. There is no right answer. The line between the sender of the email and I is already drawn by virtue of the question. My article, evidently, revealed that I could not share the same Islam as the writer. To offer a brief explanation: the Sunnis constitute the majority of Muslims worldwide. The South African *ulama* and their respective Muslim communities are informed by different theological schools of thought. While the Muslim Judicial Council (established in 1945), housed in the Western Cape, advocates a Sunni interpretation of Islam, Muslim communities in the northern (*Jamiat ul-Ulema*, established in 1934) and eastern parts (*Majlis al-Ulema*, established in 1952) of South Africa most commonly prescribe to a Deobandi-influenced faith leadership (Jardim 2015). While the 'Malay' ancestry is linked to the slaves who were imported from South and South-East Asia during the 17th century, most of the 'Indian' community members are descendants of trader immigrants who travelled from the Indian sub-continent in the 1860s (Vahed, 2006). Despite their common Islamic faith, the distinction between the Malay and Indian groups remains largely intact in contemporary Muslim societies in South Africa – not least because of the racial and ethnic classifications employed by the apartheid government, which distinguished between 'Indians' and 'coloureds' ('Malays') (Davids, 2019b). These classifications were extended into a relegation of separate residential areas and schools for 'Indian and 'coloured' families.

The Sunni interpretation of Islam consists of four schools of thought: the *Hanafi* (named after Imam Abu Hanifa), the *Maliki* (named after Imam Mālik ibn Anas), the *Shafi'i*, (named after Imam Abdullah Muhammad ibn Idris al-Shafi), and the *Hanbali* (named after Imam Ahmad ibn Hanbal). While the fundamentals pertaining to the source codes – the Qur'an and the Sunnah (example of the Prophet Muhammad PBUH) – are shared, the differences among these four schools pertain to how the four respective theologians and jurists chose to systemise Islamic law. I do not think, however, that the writer's concern had too much to do with whether I am *Hanafi* or *Shafi'i*. I suspect he might have been far more intent on labelling me as *Shia* – presuming, of course, that I shared his view that they are non-believers (made evident in his 'booklet', which I discuss below).

It is helpful to have some understanding of the long-standing historical rift between the Sunni and the *Shia* traditions. The word *Shi'i*, also referred to as *Shi'ite*, refers to a partisanship, which dates back to just after the death of the prophet Muhammad in 632 CE, and his ensuing successor. Fundamentally, the difference between the two traditions originates from the dispute surrounding the successorship of the Prophet Muhammad (PBUH). While the Sunnis conceive of leadership as a temporal domain, determined by the prevailing political climate, the Shias understand it as a divine order. In the case of the Sunnis, the rightful successors reside in the political doctrine of the Rashidun (rightly guided) caliphate, namely, Abu Bakr (ruled from 632–634 CE), Umar ibn al-Khattab (634–644 CE), Uthman ibn Affan (644–656 CE), and the fourth caliph, Ali ibn Abi Talib (656–661 CE). This reflects the political process that occurred after the death of the Prophet in 632 to select the leader by traditional tribal meeting, or *shura* (consultation). By contrast, the political doctrine of the Shi'i recognises the institution of the Imamate, or Imama, as the head of a state or community. According to this doctrine, the leader of a Muslim community, or the Imam, must be a direct descendent of Prophet Muhammad. In this instance, this refers to the son-in-law of the Prophet Muhammad (PBUH), the fourth caliph, Ali ibn Abi Talib, and his descendants alone. The Prophet (PBUH) did not have any surviving sons at the time of his death. As a result, there are several jurisprudential differences between the two traditions. While the Shias consider the sayings of Ali ibn Abi Talib as well as that of Fatima (the daughter of the Prophet, and the wife of Ali ibn Abi Talib) as equally authoritative to that of the Prophet Muhammad, the Sunnis do not.

Returning to the email itself, I chose not to respond. Other than noting that the email address indicated, 'Jamiatul Ulama Northern Cape'[18] I had no idea who had actually written the email. Whether or not I was meant to interpret this as a generalised mail from the Jamiatul Ulama, or whether the writer chose to obscure their identity out of cowardice, I do not know.

On 19 August 2018, I received another email, subject line: 'for Nuraan Davids'. This time, the mail opened with a greeting, followed by an invitation to view an attached 48-page booklet entitled 'Honouring Islam and the *Deen* by banning Muslim women from the *masaajid* [plural form of *masjid*]'.[19] The booklet, as expected, espoused entirely contradictory views to that contended in my article. Despite the writer's (who remains anonymous) initial position that my article was not 'worth a look', he spent an inordinate amount of time in trying to justify the exclusion of women from the mosque on the basis that it is better for them to remain in their homes. I do not intend to spend too much time dissecting the argument in the booklet – suffice to say that clearly the author disagrees with my views.

Scholars know and accept that criticism comes with the territory of scholarship. Hostility and derision, however, suggest a different kind of terrain, and so too, do inane comments, such as,

---

18 *Jamiatul ulama* – organisation or group of theologians
19 *Deen* refers to the way of life of Muslims; their particular practices and customs.

'No wonder, the Shariah does not accord any significance to the array of qualifications, degrees and plaudits acquired from kuffaar universities. The brains and thinking of most of these university graduates are like the *Kuffaar*. This is the effect of the educational brothels, viz. the universities and colleges.'[20] I am described as 'Acting too big for her boots', a *'shaytaan* [devil]', a non-believer, and that I 'should really feel ashamed' of myself. As these words jump from the pages, I am immediately reminded of similar hateful texts and statements, issued at the height of apartheid during the 1980s – significantly from the same kinds of organisations, namely the Jamiatul ulamas of Transvaal and Natal. Individual Muslims, and established Muslim groups, such as the Qibla, the Muslim Youth Movement (MYM), Muslim Students Association (MSA) and Call of Islam who participated in any sort of anti-apartheid activism, stood accused of being infidels. As long as Muslims could practise their faith, most Jamiatul ulamas and religious leaders did not deem it necessary (politically, socially or morally) to protest against an apartheid state.

Except for a few, explains Jardim (2015), the majority of the *ulama* adopted a 'socio-political quietism in the 1950s and 1960s, emphasising religious matters without articulating socially relevant ideas or inspiring greater political activism.'[21] In line with commonly encountered trends elsewhere, South African *ulama* interpret their roles and responsibilities as limited to mediating the theological traditions of Islam (Moosa, 1989). Their focus is on preserving a historical conservatism, which discounts any necessity to adopt any sort of political position. To provide some perspective, it was only when the roll-out of the apartheid state's Group Areas Act (no. 41 of 1950) presented a threat to the establishment of mosques, that the Muslim Judicial Council (MJC) condemned apartheid in 1961

---

20 *Kuffaar* – infidel or non-believer

21 At the time, the main Muslim organisations, who articulated a conservative political discourse were the *'u/ama-groups*, chiefly represented by the Muslim Judicial Council (MJC), the *Jamiatul 'Ulama* (Council of Theologians) of Transvaal, the *Jamiatul 'Ulama* of Natal and the *Majlisul 'Ulama* (Council of Theologians) of South Africa (Moosa, 1989).

(Bangstad 2007). In one sense, the implicit understanding among most of the *ulama* was that if 'the government allowed Muslims the religious liberty to pray, build mosques and go for pilgrimage they could not engage in *jihad* (struggle) against such an authority' (Moosa 1989: 76). In another sense, protesting against apartheid, which often involved 'co-operating with non-Muslims ... was not religiously acceptable' (Moosa, 1989: 76). Activism against apartheid, therefore, was seen as a participation in '*kufr* (infidel) politics' (Moosa, 1989: 79).

Significantly, between the period of 1970–1984, the MYM positioned itself as the most progressive Muslim organisation in the country as far as a discourse of Islam and women's rights issues was concerned (Jeenah 2006). In 1990, the MYM adopted a 'Women's Rights Campaign' as one of its three national campaigns. Among the issues identified by the campaign were: women in mosques; Muslim personal law; and women's leadership (Jeenah 2006).

Re-reading the 'booklet' for the purpose of completing the current chapter, I was struck by the same concerned imperative that motivated me to write the article years ago, namely, the countless generations of Muslim women who are socialised into an Islam in which they are (mis)led to believe that they are without agency and voice. At worst, I am subjected to contempt only through the words of an unknown male. Yes, I can choose to close my screen and shut the booklet forever. There are women, however, who endure lives of untold subjugation and humiliation because of the immersion of patriarchy into religion.

Belonging as exclusion

Patriarchy is not the sole domain of Muslim men. Patriarchy has long claimed and conquered religious and traditional discourses, certainly not only that of Islam. It is as misleading to conceive of patriarchy as a system, geared only towards the superiority of men, as it is to think that it is endorsed only by men, or that it only serves the purposes of men, or that it means the same thing at all in different contexts.

Patriarchy exists and thrives because of its dyadic relationship with women and 'others' – a relationship that is not always entirely one-sided. It is easy and true in the majority of cases that patriarchy derives its authority and power from a construction of women as de facto inferior, weak or less-than. Yet, it is also true that for most young children, patriarchy is first met on the laps, in the words and actions of mothers. While this in itself confirms the deeply entrenched machinery of patriarchy, it also reminds us that undoing patriarchy requires more than a shift in men's thinking.

As a Muslim woman, I am neither without religion, nor culture. I am also not without the patriarchal damages of my family, or my schooling, whether religious or secular. Patriarchy finds support in all these spaces, it lives as much in the language of our education, as it does in the practices of our socialisation, whether in the home or the public sphere, particularly when it involves the reproduction of existing power. It lulls women and men, alike, into a false consciousness of normality and tradition. The US political arena provides a great example of the voting power of 'white' women. Lenz (2020) reports that in the past 18 presidential elections, 'white' women have repeatedly voted for the Republican candidate, disrupting this trend only for Lyndon Johnson and for Bill Clinton's second term. As a political force, explains Lenz (2020), 'White female rage has long been better at enforcing patriarchal norms than dismantling them ... White women benefit from the status quo, while change would require burning down that system and building a new one — one where they and their children might lose the shared superiority and protection they get by being attached to powerful White men.' Retaining the status quo also allows 'white' women to cast 'others' as being responsible for societal problems and avoid their own complicity and responsibility (Lenz, 2020).

A similar false consciousness is apparent in religious interpretations. Consider, for example, the anti-feminist movement in the United States during the 1970s which was mostly based on traditional Christian values. For Christian conservatives, explains Coste (2010), feminism violates a well-known passage in the Epistles of Paul, in which Paul says: 'But I want you to understand that the head of every man is Christ, the head of a wife is her husband, and the head of Christ is God' (1 Corinthians 11:3). Today, the anti-feminist leaders of the 1970s have been replaced by a new generation of conservative women who continue the historical fight of the American Right against feminism (Coste, 2010).

Islam took root in the profoundly patriarchal setting of 7th century Arabia. It is difficult to extract this setting from the revelation of a religious text, which sought (and continues to seek) the stark oppression of women. The inherent tension between reading the Qur'an as revelation and as a historical text has yielded interpretations that might have no basis in Qur'anic exegesis – such as the oppression of women, or any other individual, for that matter. The predominance of patriarchal interpretations emanates from a broad historical convergence with multiple cultures, as Islam spread from its place of origin. These convergences implied not only an encounter with varied societally and socially specific symbolic systems, but tensions in how religion is interpreted through a cultural lens, or, how culture is interpreted through a religious lens. The location of Islam as a system of traditions, beliefs and practices in any society is not without a confluence with culture. The fluidity of a cultural influence does not only diverge and re-shape across different societies, but it also shifts within societies. Hence, what might be standard practices among Muslims in Cape Town – such as women attending the mosque – would be frowned upon or prohibited in other provinces in South Africa. There are particular historical identity formations, designated between distinct heritages of 'Indian' and 'Malay', which continue to dictate social relations and rituals, and ceremonies, such as weddings, christenings, schooling, as well as who one is allowed to marry.

Distinctions aside, whether within Islam or within the Judeo-Christian tradition, the father looms large, and is positioned on a symbolic continuum with God as Father, and hence, extended into a husband's and father's claim to rule over his wife and children (Barlas, 2002). The predominance of the father (man) has an exclusionary effect on women and their experiences – this, despite Qur'anic exegesis locating women at the centre of the family, and hence, society. Again, this understanding is not unique to Islamic theology. As Schlafly (1972: 89) shares, the Judeo-Christian tradition puts women 'on a pedestal' by virtue of the fact that 'women bear the physical consequences of the sex act, men must be required to pay in other ways. These laws and customs [of the Judeo-Christian tradition] decree that a man must carry his share by physical protection and financial support of his children and of the woman who bears his children' (Schlafly, 1972: 89). In the words of Schlafly (1972: 93): 'Why should we lower ourselves to 'equal rights' when we already have the status of special privilege?'

For Muslim women, who enjoy the privileges of being taken care of, their understanding is no different to that of Schlafly's (1972), even when they recognise that their status as a daughter, wife, and mother, does not necessarily translate into their inclusion as women. 'Interpretations of the textual sources, applications of those interpretations when constructing laws to govern personal and private Islamic affairs and to construct public policies and institutions to control Islamic policies and authority', explains Wadud (2006: 22), are based upon male-interpretive privilege. Further entrenching this male-interpretive privilege, however, is the unfortunate reality that although Muslim women directly experience the consequences of oppressive misreadings of religious texts, few question their legitimacy, and fewer still have explored the liberatory aspects of the Qur'an's teachings (Barlas, 2002). In the absence of reading and critically engaging with the paradigmatic foundations of their own faith, women are neither able to contest oppressive or contradictory readings, nor are they able to (re)insert themselves into the agential roles of their own religious frameworks. As a result, while there are women who are prepared to contest their exclusion or marginalisation within mosques, there are as many, who either because of complacency, or a lack of interest and understanding, are unconcerned about whether or not they can actively participate in religious spaces. Maybe they prefer not to be bothered to make their way to the mosque, maybe they do not extend their exclusion into a broader patriarchal narrative, or maybe their experiences of a patriarchal climate are so entrenched and normalised, that they are incapable of seeing its flaws.

In the absence of direct engagements with a large sample of Muslim women, it is impossible to claim an informed understanding on why there seemingly is silence from most women on the unjust treatment of women in Islam. However, my own experiences – of which only one is shared in this chapter – allow me to have some understanding of the thickness of patriarchy among South African Muslims. It is a thickness that immediately conceives and relegates any contrary thinking to a liminal 'outsider' space.

It is possible, as I have learnt through my lived experiences, that belonging to a particular identity or community group does not need to infer a consistency of attachment. It is acceptable, perhaps even necessary, to occupy identities with a margin of detachment, a willingness to step away from what those identities might suggest, whether by their imagery, associations or presentations. The content of this chapter has nothing to do with the degrees of my faith. It has to do with the lived misinterpretations of a religious framework. If I am to remain true to this framework, then it is necessary for me to *be* within my faith. This, as I understand it, requires me, at times, to be simultaneously attached to and detached from my faith community. I am part of a collective, yet I am also an individual within that collective.

A community offers belonging, an unencumbered warm embrace of acceptance and inclusion; yet it also has conditions, framed by certain norms, customs, traditions and rituals. As a member of a faith community, I am expected to step into these norms, allowing me access to the benefits of belonging. But laying claim to a particular faith also requires me to be bear witness to who I am, what I believe, why I believe what I do, and how my beliefs are made manifest through me. The premise of witnessing occupies a profound centrality in Islam, inviting those who believe into perpetual spiritually contractual enactments of bearing testimony to what they believe. Muslims are called into a testimony of faith: 'I bear witness that there is no god, but God, and that the Prophet Muhammad (PBUH) is the final Messenger'. They are also summoned to continually engage critically with what they believe, ensure that they live it, and to question it as they see fit. Hence, the iterative Qur'anic reminders to believers to think, ponder, reflect, and contemplate their faith (see 4: 82; 13: 3; 30: 8), as well as to exercise reason and logic (see 4: 174; 8: 22; 21: 30). I have to afford myself the right to lean outward in order to have a wider vantage point of what is happening inside. It is when we are completely immersed in a community or society, that we lose our ability to truly *see* that community. Our lack of distance engulfs us into its folds, its embraces, its ways, which are all good and inviting, but also prevents us from seeing the kinks and bruises.

Un-living patriarchy

What is this community of which I am part, the one into which I have been inserted by virtue of my birth into a Muslim family? It originates from two different ancestral homes – a difference noted by apartheid's division between 'coloured' and 'Indian'. Despite forcing families into different residential areas through the Group Areas Act, despite forcing children into 'Indian' and 'coloured' designated schools, and despite enduring cultural differences (as already alluded to in this chapter), Muslim communities in South Africa are bound by at least two factors. One is their shared faith, and the other is their common experience of apartheid's dehumanising laws. As an ethnic marker, being Muslim was seen as separate from the wider label of 'coloured' (Jeppie, 2001). Residential clustering made it easy for Muslims to establish mosques and *madrassahs*, and to practise their religious beliefs without interference from the state (Vahed,

2006). This freedom spilled over into the establishment of Moslem Mission schools – a response to the non-accommodation of Muslim children and their beliefs.

Between 1948 and 1990, all public schools prescribed Christian National Education (CNE). Derived from a distinctive interpretation of Calvinism, CNE propagated an inseparability between the church and the state. Public schools were inherently 'Christian', which meant that all school going children, regardless of their religious backgrounds, or whether they ascribed to any religion at all, were expected to participate in their schools' Christian ethos. In practical terms, this meant Christian prayers being recited at the commencement and conclusion of the school day; before break-times; before examinations; before sporting events; and before school assemblies, which included the singing of a hymn. It also meant the propagation of 'white' supremacy through the public school system.

The apartheid state supported and subsidised Moslem Mission schools because these schools ensured a further separation between faith communities, feeding into the state's meta-narrative of entrenching segregated communities.

For a number of Muslim communities, the cloistered pockets of isolation enforced through apartheid meant a preservation of traditions, rituals, and a way of life, which became perceived as being under threat once South Africa transitioned to a democracy. The introduction of a democracy shifted historically marginalised and oppressed communities into an unfamiliar status of equal citizenship and, most importantly, it opened an unequivocal set of rights of responsibilities, confirming individual autonomy and agency.

While welcomed and celebrated by most South Africans, the country's liberal Constitution created unintended tensions within certain communities. For most Muslim communities, the legalisation of abortion, gambling and pornography are seen as irreconcilable with an Islamic worldview. This tension became especially apparent amid calls for the boycotting of the country's first democratic elections, in April 1994, by the Islamic Unity Convention.

Seemingly, inasmuch as most Muslims are in agreement about the fundamental injustices perpetuated by an apartheid regime, there continues to be an uncertainty and reticence in engaging across historically divided lines. While it is possible to make sense of this hesitancy in relation to the suddenness of these changes, particularly in the education environment, it is hard to ignore the equally sudden turn of Muslim communities, as well as other faith communities, into renewed forms of retreat and insulation. To Vawda (2017: 34), many Muslims in South Africa began to focus on 'values of piety and morality, rather than continue to engage in the larger public debates about recognition of cultural differences and the relevance of Islam in times of continued inequality, nation building, reconciliation, reconstruction and development'.

I find myself as part of a community that probably became more distinctive within its own understandings and framings after apartheid ceased. Because of the laws of apartheid, they were a de facto separated, but close-knit community. Under democracy, they have had to find new ways of defining that separation. This is clear not only in separated schooling for an increasing number of Muslim children, but also community media stations and channels, and Islamic-based political parties. While indicative of a pluralist and democratic society, there are also associated nuances of retreat and insularity. Again, none of this is unusual for faith communities, as they endeavour to foster membership solidarity through preserving religious identities and practices. Questions and concerns, however, arise when these identity-specific structures and practices are resistant to critique.

Benhabib's (2011: 68) description of the Muslim female body as the site of 'symbolic confrontations between a re-essentialised understanding of religious and cultural differences and the forces of state power' was written against the background of *l'affaire du foulard* (the scarf affair) in France.[22] According to Benhabib (2011), the nature of the tension between religion as a political theology and the forces of state power can, at best, be described as a clash between identities of a collective nature (as envisaged by the nation-state) and identities of an individual nature (as manifested in different religions and cultures). As a result of this conflict, Muslim women are torn between entering the public square on stipulated conditions and retreating to the private sphere, where they can be who they are. Quite profoundly, it is possible to extend this exact same argument into the treatment of Muslim women with regards to their public participation in the mosque – only this time, the treatment is not meted out by liberal democracies, but by Muslim men. It is not just that Muslim women's historical activism and contributions have been excluded from mainstream Islamic interpretations; it is also that this exclusion has allowed a male-interpretive privilege to dominate the governance of personal and private Muslim affairs (Wadud, 2006). To this end, says Barlas (2002: 12–13), 'Patriarchy is a historically specific mode of rule by fathers that, in its religious and traditional forms, assumes a real as well as symbolic continuum between the 'Father/fathers', that is, between a patriachalised view of God as Father/male, and a theory of father-right, extending to the husband's claim to rule over his wife and children' – thereby inscribing indelible gendered practices as unquestionable norms.

Gender, contends Butler (1999: 5), is not always composed coherently or consistently in different historical contexts. Gender intersects with social, class, ethnic, sexual and regional modalities of discursively comprised identities. To her, the political assumption that there must be a collective or universal basis for feminism is often conflated with a similar assumption that the oppression of women is singular in nature. Implicit in this assumption of singularity of

---

[22] Benhabib analyses the Scarf Affair, which began in France in 1989. It traces the events initiated by three Muslim high school students whose insistence on wearing headscarves to school placed them in conflict first with their school and eventually the French state and judiciary. Wearing the scarves was seen as a direct challenge to the French educational system's fundamental principle of *laïcité*.

experience is the belief that women own a singular identity regardless of culture, religion, class or race. Yet, the struggles of women are as layered and varied as their identities. The same women, who might enjoy equal recognition and opportunity in the workplace, might encounter discrimination in their faith space. The continuing exclusion and marginalisation of Muslim women emanates from two internodal points: the presumption of male authority in the interpretation of scripture, and hence, the presumption of androcentrism over the public domain, including sacred spaces. In response, Muslim feminists have made convincing arguments that the patriarchal representation of the family does not concur with the Qur'anic principles of human equality and gender justice (Badran, 2009).

Postcolonial feminist theorising on religion has revealed the dominance of patriarchal norms informing women's roles and relationships in religious traditions (Hoel, 2013a). By placing believing women's experiences at the heart of their analysis, explains Hoel (2013a: 73), 'feminist scholars of religion have not only rendered visible the androcentrism that underpins religious frameworks but also developed gender-inclusive methodological paradigms that are notably absent from mainstream religious scholarly theorising.' In this regard, Muslim feminists do not locate the spheres of public and private on opposite ends of a continuum. Instead, Badran (2009) explains, by supporting an egalitarian model of both family and society, Islamic feminists promote a more flowing public–private continuum of gender equality. This continuum not only discards the public–private division, but also insists upon gender equality within the religious domain of the public sphere. Fundamentally, it is gender equality and gender justice, as promulgated by the very foundational sources of Islam that can undo and transcend androcentric discourses and dominations.

Feminists do not only take into account the contextual situatedness of Islam, but, says Mirza (2008), they also assert that the work of women, who had played a significant role as the creators of oral texts, became invisible after the inception of Islam, both as originators and interpreters of such texts. Scriptural literature as well as legal texts were reinscribed with a masculine bias, resulting in the atrophying of the egalitarian ethos of Islam (Mirza, 2008). Dismantling and discarding this ethos is possible by, on the one hand, disrupting traditional notions of authority, and resisting the orthodoxy of patriarchy. And on the other hand, by deconstructing gendered Islamic discourses, and producing interpretations of scripture that can be utilised for the radical re-configuration of gendered legal rights (Mirza, 2008). This approach in no way infers a departure from the paradigmatic foundations of Islam. What this approach demands is renewed engagements with the source codes – by all Muslims – and for a return to the socially just pulse of Islam in its authenticity.

8

Postscript: Through the doorway

I conclude this book with a consciousness that there will always be more to say about racism, 'othering', marginalisation, exclusion, oppression and humiliation. The world, as we know it, will always be in a state of 'othering' and, as such, will never be without hegemonies of power delineated along entrenchments of centres and margins. We live in a world, says Santos (2018), in which the most repugnant forms of social inequality and discrimination are becoming politically acceptable. People and groups relegated to the margins live in a perpetual state of epistemic violence where their inflicted subjugation morphs from one form into another. Similarly, there are boundless and inexhaustible conceptions and enactments of diversity not only across and in civilizations but within individuals. Postcolonialism, therefore, can have no end because we have yet to adequately capture and articulate epistemologies which take us out of Western essentialism and exceptionalism, and into a new kind of world in which racial, social and cultural subjugation of any people becomes antithetical to the very idea of what makes us human.

As I have tried to reflect through my own experiences, there are certain ways in which the world not only functions but legitimises itself through its own actions. Knowledge is used and reproduced so that existing dominant structures are repeatedly endorsed – to the extent that any difference, whether in the form of gender, culture, race, religion or language is not seen as lived expressions of diversity but as unreachable, irreconcilable and, hence, something to be suppressed and disregarded. And yet, it is in turning towards difference and being open to it that we can shift in who we potentially can be. It is through our engagement with diverse expressions of lives that we can cross over into other worlds and other knowledge forms. All knowledges, states Santos (2018: 33), 'are testimonies since what they know of reality (their active dimension) is always reflected back in what they reveal about the subject of this knowledge (their subjective dimension.' It is easy for some of us to proclaim that the world is not of our making, that it was like this – bent and disfigured – long before our arrival into it. But every single time we remain silent in the face of these disfigurements we contribute to how this world is. In our preference for silence and complacency, the risk always is that, in the end, the world would not only have made us but undone us in its making.

It takes hard work to push against existing structures of inequality and exclusion, as might be encountered in schools and universities, or any other institution. These organisations often hide behind the very notion of their structuredness as a justification of their norms. Phrases such as 'our way' or 'this is how it has always been done' need intensive deconstruction both in terms of whose ways need to be retained and whose ways need to be excluded. The subtleties of language cannot be underestimated. Language, after all, is never without power. In many ways, therefore, it is easier to confront systems of inequality rather than trying to confront individual privileges. It is easier to get people to talk about the systemic reproduction of inequality than to get the same people to reflect upon their individual role in relation to that reproduction, and hence their own privilege. Why would anyone want to relinquish their privilege? Any yet it seems clear that if inequalities, marginalisation and 'othering' are to be confronted and disrupted then this can only happen with individuals as the starting point.

As individuals, we are always 'turned' towards others, because the other is already turning towards us, waiting for us to listen, to hear their cries and act with compassion (Derrida, 1988). In this regard, says, Haraway (1988: 579–580), 'we do need an earth-wide network of connections, including the ability partially to translate knowledges among very different – and power-differentiated communities. We need the power of modern critical theories of how meanings and bodies get made, not in order to deny meanings and bodies, but in order to build meanings and bodies that have a chance for life.'

I conclude with a knowledge and hope that in writing this book I have offered some meaning not only to my own lived experiences, but that I have reminded all of us that who we are is never without meaning. As a collective, even in our estranged lives, we have it within ourselves to find a way towards cultivating a world of mutual regard. The challenge is to push through and disrupt the exclusion, marginalisation, humiliation and pain. It's the only way to emerge on the other side. In the end, this is probably the best way to describe what it means to be and live a postcolonial life. It is neither a state of arrival nor does it present any assurances of recognition, inclusion or belonging. What it offers is a hopeful avenue of sense-making, a rupturing of a world intent on lines, borders and hierarchies.

References

Abdelgadir A & Fouka V (2020) Political secularism and Muslim integration in the west: Assessing the effects of the French headscarf ban. *American Political Science Review* 114(3): 707–723

Achinstein B, Ogawa RT, Sexton D & Freitas C (2010) Retaining teachers of color: A pressing problem and a potential strategy for 'hard-to-staff' schools. *Review of Educational Research* 80(1): 71–107

Adhikari M (2004) 'Not black enough': Changing expressions of Coloured identity in post-apartheid South Africa. *South African Historical Journal* 51: 167–178

Adhikari M (ed.) (2013) *Burdened by Race: Coloured identities in southern Africa*. UCT Press

Afsaruddin A (2005) Muslim views on education: Parameters, purview, and possibilities. *Journal of Catholic Legal Studies* 44(143): 143–178

Ahmed L (1992) *Women and Gender in Islam: Historical roots of a modern debate*. Yale University Press

Ahmed S (1997) Intimate touches: Proximity and distance in international feminist dialogues. *Oxford Literary Review* 19(1/2): 19–46

Ahmed S (2003) The politics of fear in the making of worlds. *International Journal of Qualitative Studies in Education* 16(3): 377–398

Ahmed S (2004) Declarations of whiteness: The non-performativity of anti-racism. *Borderlands* 3(2): 104–126

Ahmed S (2006) The nonperformativity of antiracism. *Meridians* 7(1): 104–126

Ahmed S (2007) A phenomenology of whiteness. *Feminist Theory* 8(2): 149–168

Ahmed S & Swan E (2006) Doing diversity. *Policy Futures in Education* 4(2): 96–100

Alcalde MA & Subramaniam M (2020) Women in leadership: Challenges and recommendations. *Inside HigherEd*. https://www.insidehighered.com/views/2020/07/17/women-leadership-academe-still-face-challenges-structures-systems-and-mind-sets

Al-Qaradawi Y (1982) *The Lawful and the Prohibited in Islam*. American Trust

Alvesson M (2003) Methodology for close up studies: Struggling with closeness and closure. *Higher Education* 46: 167–193

Ampofo-Anti OY (2019) Equality Court prohibits display of old South African flag. *GroundUp*. https://www.groundup.org.za/article/old-south-african-flag-constitutes-hate-speech-says-equality-court/

Anderson L (2006) Analytic autoethnography. *Journal of Contemporary Ethnography* 35(4): 373–395

Appiah KA (2015) Race in the modern world: The problem of the color line. *Foreign Affairs* 94(2): 1–8

Applebaum B (2008) 'Doesn't my experience count?' White students, the authority of experience and social justice pedagogy. *Race Ethnicity and Education* 11(4): 405–414

Auda J (2017) *Reclaiming the Mosque: The role of women in Islam's House of Worship*. Claritas

Badran M (2009) Feminism in Islam: Secular and religious convergences. Oneworld

Bangstad S (2007) *Global Flows, Local Appropriations: Facets of secularisation and re-Islamization among contemporary Cape Muslims*. Amsterdam University Press

Barkley Brown E (2006) 'What has happened here': The politics of difference in women's history and feminist politics. *Feminist Studies* 18(2): 295–312

Barlas A (2002) *Believing Women in Islam: Unreading patriarchal interpretations of the Qur'an*. University of Texas Press

Barthes R (1977) *The Death of the Author: Image, music, text* (tr. S Heath). Hill & Wang. pp. 142–148

Battersby J (2005) Re-inscribing race and ethnicity in post-apartheid South Africa. In: P Gervais-Lambony, F Landy & S Oldfield (eds) *Reconfiguring Identities and Building Territories in India and South Africa*. Centre de Sciences Humaines. pp. 85–97

Benhabib S (2011) *Dignity in Adversity: Human rights in troubled times*. Polity

Bernal DD (2002) Critical race theory, Latino critical theory, and critical raced-gendered epistemologies: Recognising students of color as holders and creators of knowledge. *Qualitative Inquiry* 8(1): 105–126

Bhabha HK (1994) *The Location of Culture*. Routledge

Bhambra GK (2014) Postcolonial and decolonial dialogues. *Postcolonial Studies* 17(2): 115–121

Bochner A. (2007) Notes toward an ethics of memory in autoethnography. In NK Denzin & MD Giardina (eds), *Ethical Futures in Qualitative Research: Decolonizing the politics of knowledge* (pp. 197–208). Left Coast Press

Butler J (1999) *Gender Trouble: Feminism and the subversion of identity*. Routledge

Carrim N (2001) From teachers to educators: Homogenising tendencies in contemporary South African educational reforms. *International Journal of Educational Development* 21: 45–52

Clark NL & Worger WH (2004) *South Africa: The rise and fall of apartheid*. Pearson Education

Connelly FM & Clandinin DJ (1990) Stories of experience and narrative inquiry. *Educational Researcher* 19(5): 2–14

Cooke M, Ahmad F, Badran M, Moallem M & Zine J (2008) Roundtable Discussion: Deploying the Muslimwoman. *Journal of Feminist Studies* in Religion 24(1): 91–99

Coste F (2010) Conservative women and feminism in the United States: Between hatred and appropriation. *Caliban* 27: 167–176

Das V (2007) *Life and Words: Violence and the descent into the ordinary.* University of California Press

Davids N (2016) Religion, culture, and the exclusion of Muslim women: On finding a reimagined form of inclusive-belonging. *Knowledge Cultures* 4(4): 46–59

Davids N (2018a) How Muslims betray Islam by not allowing women in the mosques. *News24*. https://www.news24.com/news24/columnists/guestcolumn/how-muslims-betray-islam-by-not-allowingwomen-in-mosques-20180607

Davids N (2018b) Global citizenship education, postcolonial identities, and a moral imagination. In: I Davis, A Peterson, D Kiwan, C Peck, E Sant, L Ho & Y Waghid (eds) *Palgrave Handbook of Global Citizenship and Education*. Palgrave Macmillan. pp. 193–208

Davids N (2018c) Democratic citizenship education: An opportunity for the re-negotiation of teacher identity in South African schools. *Education as Change* 22(1): 1–17

Davids N (2019a) You are not like us: On teacher exclusion, imagination, and disrupting perception. *Journal of Philosophy of Education* 53(1): 165–179

Davids N (2019b) Muslim education in democratic South Africa: Convergence or divergence of religion and citizenship? *Journal of Education in Muslim Societies* 1(1): 44–59

Davids N (2019c) Schools as restorative spaces for democratic citizenship education. *Journal of Education* 77: 79–93

Davids N (2020a) The controversy of Muslim women in liberal democracies. In: K Hytten (ed.) *The Oxford Encyclopedia of Philosophy of Education*. Oxford University Press

Davids N (2020b) Governance in South African schools: Democratic advancement or hindrance? *Educational Management Administration & Leadership* 1–16

Davids N & Waghid Y (2015) The invisible silence of race: On exploring some experiences of minority group teachers at South African schools. *Power and Education* 7(2): 155–168

Deem R & Morley L (2006) Diversity in the academy? Staff perceptions of equality policies in six contemporary higher education institutions. *Policy Futures in Education* 4(2): 185–202

Delamont S (2009) The only honest thing: Autoethnography, reflexivity and small crises in fieldwork. *Ethnography and Education* 4: 51–63

Delgado R & Stefanicic J (eds) (1995) *Critical Race Theory: The cutting edge*. Temple University Press

De Oliveira Andreotti V & De Souza LMTM (2012) Introduction: (Towards) global citizenship education 'otherwise'. In: V De Oliveira Andreotti & LMTM De Souza (eds) *Postcolonial Perspectives on Global Citizenship Education*. Routledge. pp. 1–8

Department of Education (DoE) (1994) *A Policy Framework for Education and Training*. Government Printers

Department of Education (DoE) (1996) *South African Schools Act of 1996*. Government Printers

Department of Higher Education and Training (DHET) (2019) *Employment Equity Policy*. Government Printers

Derrida J (1988) The politics of friendship. *Journal of Philosophy* 85(11): 632–648

Ellis C & Bochner AP (2000) Autoethnography, personal narrative, reflexivity. In: NK Denzin & YS Lincoln (eds) *Handbook of Qualitative Research* (2nd edn). Sage. pp. 733–768

Ellis C, Adams TE & Bochner AP (2011) Autoethnography: An overview. *Historical Social Research* 36(4): 273–290

Erasmus Z (2001) Re-imagining coloured identities in post-apartheid South Africa. In: Z Erasmus (ed.) *Coloured by History, Shaped by Place: New perspectives on coloured identities in Cape Town*. Kwela. pp. 13–28

Erasmus Z (2017) *Race Otherwise, Forging a New Humanism for South Africa*. Wits University Press

Esposito JL & DeLong-Bas N (2001) *Women in Muslim Family Law*. Syracuse University Press

Farber D & Sherry S (1995) Telling stories out of school: An essay on legal narratives. *Stanford Law Review* 45(4): 807–855

Fielding-Singh P, M Devon & B Swethaa (2018, 28 August) Why women stay out of the spotlight at work. *Harvard Business Review*

Fokazi S (2018) 'I want my daughters to grow up in an inclusive environment': Parents speak out on 'racism' at Cape school. *TimesLIVE*. https://www.timeslive.co.za/news/south-africa/2018-11-07-iwant-my-daughters-to-grow-up-in-an-inclusive-environmentparents-speak-out-on-alleged-racism-at-cape-school/

Geertz C (1973) *The Interpretation of Culture*. Basic

Ghafournia N (2020) Negotiating gendered religious space: Australian Muslim women and the mosque. *Religions* 11(686): 1–17

Golnaraghi G & Dye K (2016) Discourses of contradiction: A postcolonial analysis of Muslim women and the veil. *International Journal of Cross Cultural Management* 16(2): 137–152

Hammett D (2010) Ongoing contestations: the use of racial signifiers in post-apartheid South Africa. *Social Identities* 16(2): 247–260

Haraway D (1988) Situated knowledges: The science question in feminism and the privilege of partial perspective. *Feminist Studies* 14(3): 575–599

Hargreaves J (2000) *Heroines of Sport: The politics of difference and identity*. Routledge

Hartman S (2008) Venus in two acts. *Small Axe* 12, 2(26): 1–14

Hoel N (2013a) Feminism and religion and the politics of location: Situating Islamic feminism in South *Africa. Journal of Gender and Religion in Africa* 19(2): 73–89

Hoel N (2013b) Sexualising the sacred, sacralising sexuality: An analysis of public responses to Muslim women's religious leadership *in the Context of a Cape Town Mosque. Journal for the Study of Religion* 26(2): 25–41

Holman Jones S (2005) Autoethnography: Making the personal political. In: NK Denzin & YS Lincoln (eds) *Handbook of Qualitative Research*. pp. 763–791. Sage

hooks b (2004) Understanding patriarchy. *Imagine No Borders*. https://imaginenoborders.org/pdf/zines/UnderstandingPatriarchy.pdf

Huett S & Goodman D (2014) Alterity. In: T Teo (ed.) *Encyclopedia of Critical Psychology*. Springer. https://doi.org/10.1007/978-1-4614-5583-7_13

Hussain F (ed.) (1984) *Muslim Women*. St. Martin's Press

Ingersoll R, May H & Collins G (2019) Recruitment, employment, retention and the minority teacher shortage. *Education Policy Analysis Archives* 27(37): 1–37

Isaacs L (2018) Parents For Change wants department to take concerns seriously. *IOL*. https://www.iol.co.za/capetimes/news/parents-for-change-wants-department-to-take-concerns-seriously-17805918

Jansen JD (2004) Race and education after ten years. *Perspectives in Education* 22(4): 117–128

Jansen JD (2007) Learning and leading in a globalized world: The lessons from South Africa. In: T Townsend & R Bates (eds) *Handbook of Teacher Education: Globalization, standards and professionalism in times of change*. Springer. pp. 25–40

Jardim G (2015) Muslim women against apartheid: Muslim women for universal values. *The Journal of Scriptural Reasoning* 14(1). https://jsr.shanti.virginia.edu/back-issues/vol-14-number-1-june-2015-politics-scripture-and war/muslim-women-against-apartheid-muslim-women-for-universal-values/

Jeenah N (2006) The national liberation struggle and Islamic feminisms in South Africa. *Women's Studies International Forum* 29: 27–41

Jeppie MS (2001) Introduction: Reclassifications: Coloured, Malay, Muslim. In: Z Erasmus (ed.) *Coloured by History, Shaped by Place: New perspectives on Coloured identities in Cape Town*. Kwela. pp. 80–96

Jones C (2006) Falling between the cracks: What diversity means for black women in higher education. *Policy Futures in Education* 4(2): 145–159

Khiabany G & Williamson M (2008) Veiled bodies–Naked racism: Culture, politics and race in the sun. *Race & Class* 50(2): 69–88

Kirmani N (2009) Deconstructing and reconstructing "Muslim women" through women's narratives. *Journal of Gender Studies* 18(1): 47–62

Kohli R & Pizarro M (2016) Fighting to educate our own: Teachers of color, relational accountability, and the struggle for racial justice. *Equity & Excellence in Education* 49(1): 72–84

Ladson-Billings G (2000) Racialized discourses and ethnic epistemologies. In: NK Denzin & YS Lincoln (eds) *Handbook of Qualitative Research* (2nd edn). pp. 257–277). Sage

Le Grange L (2021) (Individual) responsibility in decolonising the university curriculum. *South African Journal of Higher Education* 35(1): 1–17

Lelyveld J (1986) *Move your Shadow: South Africa, black and white*. Times

Lenz L (2020, 27 November) White women vote Republican. Get used to it, Democrats. *Washington Post*. https://www.washingtonpost.com/opinions/2020/11/27/white-women-vote-republican-get-used-itdemocrats/

Lewicki A & O'Toole T (2017) Acts and practices of citizenship: Muslim women's activism in the UK. *Ethnic and Racial Studies* 40(1): 152–171

Lugones MC & Spelman EV (1983) *Have we got a theory for you! Feminist theory, cultural imperialism and the demand for 'the woman's voice'*. *Women's Studies International Forum* 6(6): 573–581

Lugones M (2016) *The coloniality of gender*. In: W Harcourt (eds) *The Palgrave Handbook of Gender and Development: Critical engagements in feminist theory and practice*. Palgrave Macmillan. pp. 13–33

Mahmood S (2005) *The Politics of Piety. The Islamic Revival and the Feminist Subject*. Princeton University Press

Maldonado-Torres N (2016) Outline of ten theses on coloniality and decoloniality. Foundation Frantz Fanon. http://frantzfanonfoundation-fondationfrantzfanon.com/article2360.html

Mancini S (2012) Patriarchy as the exclusive domain of the other: The veil controversy, false projection and cultural racism. *International Journal of Constitutional Law* 10(2): 411–428

Masschelein J & Simons M (2013) *In Defense of the School: A public issue* (tr. J McMartin). E-ducation, Culture & Society Publishers

Masweneng K (2018) 'We want to pray in mosques too,' says a group of Muslim women. *TimesLIVE*. https://www.timeslive.co.za/news/south-africa/2018-06-06-we-want-to-pray-in-mosquestoo-says-a-group-of-muslim-women/

Matsuda MJ (1992) When the first quail calls: Multiple consciousness as jurisprudential method. *Women's Rights Law Reporter* 213: 1–5

McGregor M (2013) The chaos of 'Bantu' education. *Leaves from my Logbook: Murray McGregor's missionary and maritime memories* [Blog]. https://murraymcgregor.wordpress.com/chapter-15-the-chaos-of %e2%80%9cbantu%e2%80%9d education/

McKinney C (2010) Schooling in black and white: Assimilationist discourses and subversive identity performances in a desegregated South African girls' school. *Race, Ethnicity and Education* 13(2): 191–207

Mernissi F (1991) *The Veil and the Male Elite: A feminist interpretation of women's rights in Islam*. Blackwell

Mirza HS (2006) Transcendence over diversity: Black women in the academy. *Policy Futures in Education* 4(2): 101–113

Mirza HS (2013) 'A second skin': Embodied intersectionality, transnationalism and narratives of identity and belonging among Muslim women in Britain. *Women's Studies International Forum* 36: 5–15

Mirza Q (2008) Islamic feminism and gender equality. *ISIM Review* 21: 30–31

Mohanty C (1988) Under western eyes: Feminist scholarship and colonial discourses. *Feminist Review* 30: 61–88

Mohanty CT (1984) Under western eyes: Feminist scholarship and colonial discourses. *Boundary* 2, 12/13 (3/1): 333–358

Mohanty R & Tandon R (2006) Identity, exclusion, inclusion: Issues in participatory citizenship. In: R Mohanty & R Tandon (eds) *Participatory Citizenship: Identity, exclusion, inclusion*. Sage. pp. 9–28

Moloi K (2007) An overview of education management in South Africa. *South African Journal of Education* 27(3): 463–476

Moosa E (1989) Muslim conservatism in South Africa. *Journal of Theology for Southern Africa* 69: 73–81

Morgan MJ (ed.) (2009) *The Impact of 9/11 and the New Legal Landscape: The day that changed everything?* Palgrave Macmillan

Murad AH (2020) *Travelling Home: Essays on Islam in Europe*. Quilliam Press

Naidoo S, Pillay J & Conley LN (2018) The management and governance of racial integration in public secondary schools in Gauteng. *KOERS — Bulletin for Christian Scholarship* 83(1): 1–13

Nas A *(2021)* "Women in mosques": Mapping the gendered religious space through online activism. *Feminist Media Studies*. 10.1080/14680777.2021.1878547

Nel N, Wang L, Krog S & Lebeloane LDM (2019) A collaborative auto-ethnography: A South Africa-China community of practice and its international collaborative research process. *Education as Change* 23(1): 1–22

News24 (2018) Rustenburg girls alumni in open letter: 'We were forced to become more white'. https://www.news24.com/news24/SouthAfrica/News/rustenburg-alumni-in-open-letter-wewere-forced-to-become-more-white-20181106

Ngcobo T & Tikly L (2008) Key dimensions of effective leadership for change: A focus on township and rural schools in South Africa. Paper presented at CCEAM 2008, ICC Durban, 8–12 September

Nyhagen L (2019) Mosques as gendered spaces: The complexity of women's compliance with, and resistance to, dominant gender norms, and the importance of male allies. *Religions* 10(321): 1–15

Orwell G (1946) Why I write. https://orwell.ru/library/essays/wiw/english/e_wiw

Orwell G (2017) *On Truth*. Harvill Secker

Pampallis J (2003) Education reform and school choice in South Africa: A cautionary tale in choosing choice. In: D Plank & G Sykes (eds) *Choosing Choice: School choice in international perspective*. Teachers College. pp. 143–163

Pather R (2018a) Cape school accused of coercing black teacher to resign. *Mail&Guardian*. https://mg.co.za/article/2018-11-02-00-are-black-teachers-real-teachers/

Pather R (2018b) Parents, W Cape education department clash over Rustenburg school racism allegations. *Mail&Guardian*. https://mg.co.za/article/2018-11-05-parents-w-cape-education-department-clash-over-rustenburg-school-racism-allegations/

Peters MA (2019) Interview with George Yancy, African-American philosopher of critical philosophy of race. *Educational Philosophy and Theory* 51(7): 663–669

Petzen J (2012) Contesting Europe: A call for an anti-modern sexual politics. *European Journal of Women's Studies* 19(1): 97–114

Pillay D, Naicker I & Pithouse-Morgan K (eds) (2016) *Academic Autoethnographies: Inside teaching in higher education*. Sense

Poerwandari EK (2021) Minimizing bias and maximizing the potential strengths of autoethnography as a narrative research. *Japanese Psychological Research* 63(4): 310–323

Pyke KD (2010) What is internalized racial oppression and why don't we study it? Acknowledging racism's hidden injuries. *Sociological Perspectives* 53(4): 551–572

Radcliffe S (1994) (Representing) Post-colonial women: Authority, difference and feminisms. *Area* 26 (1): 25–32

Santos BD (2007) Beyond abyssal thinking: From global lines to ecologies of knowledges. *Review* 30(1): 45–89

Santos BD (2018) *The End of the Cognitive Empire: The coming of age of epistemologies of the South*. Duke University Press

Schlafly P (1972) What's wrong with equal rights for women? https://awpc.cattcenter.iastate.edu/2016/02/02/whats-wrong-with-equal-rights-for-women-1972/#:~:text=This%20speech%20began%20as%20an,woman%20is%20the%20most%20privileged

Scott JW (1991) The evidence of experience. *Critical Inquiry* 17(Summer): 773–797

Shofia N (2020) Why veil? Religious headscarves and the public role of women. https://drive.google.com/file/d/17VMaOGLeshTSGdWTa7SmM_AlVJkEXF7A/view

Shohat E (1992) Notes on the 'postcolonial'. *Social Text* 31/32: 99–113

Sian K (2014) Boaventura de Sousa Santos. In: K Sian (ed.) *In Conversations in Postcolonial Thought*. Palgrave Macmillan. pp. 63–80

Sium A, Desai C & Ritskes E (2012) Towards the 'tangible unknown': Decolonization and the indigenous future. *Decolonization: Indigeneity, Education & Society 1(1)*: 1–13

Soudien C & McKinney C (2016) The character of the multicultural education discussion in South Africa. In: J Lo Bianco & A Bal (eds) *Learning from Difference: Comparative accounts of multicultural education*. Springer. pp. 125–145

Soudien C & Sayed Y (2004) A new racial state? Exclusion and inclusion in education: policy and practice in South Africa, Perspectives in Education 22(4): 101–115

Southall R (2020) South Africa's main opposition party *caught in an unenviable political* bind. News24. https://www.news24.com/news24/columnists/guestcolumn/opinion-the-cape-independence-debate-should-the-da-be-renamed-the-undemocratic-alliance-20201214

Sparkes AC (2007) Embodiment, academics, and the audit culture: A story seeking consideration. *Qualitative Research* 7(4): 521–550

Spivak GC (1988) Can the subaltern speak? In: C Nelson & L Grossberg (eds) *Marxism and Interpretation of Culture*. University of Illinois Press. pp. 24–32

Spivak GC (2005) Scattered speculations on the subaltern and the popular. *Postcolonial Studies* 8(4): 475–486

Spivak GC & Grosz E (1990) Criticism, feminism, and the institution. In: S Harasym (ed.) *Gayatri Chakravorty Spivak: The Post-colonial Critic. Interviews, strategies, dialogues*. Routledge. pp. 1–16

Spivak GC, Hutnyk J, McQuire S & Papastergiadis N (1990) Strategy, identity, writing. In: S Harasym (ed.) *Gayatri Chakravorty Spivak: The Post-colonial Critic*. Routledge. pp. 35–49

Stellenbosch University (2021) Human Resources. http://www.sun.ac.za/english/human-resources/employment-equity-and-diversity

Tayob A (2011) Islamization for South African Muslim independent schools. In: A Tayob, I Niehaus & W Weisse (eds) *Muslim Schools and Education in Europe and South Africa*. Waxmann. pp. 39–54

Tedlock B (2000) Ethnography and ethnographic representation. In: NK Denzin & YS Lincoln (eds), *Handbook of Qualitative Research*, (2nd edn). Sage. pp. 455–486

Tewolde AI (2020) Am I Black, am I Coloured, am I Indian? An autoethnographic account of a refugee's everyday encounters with ascribed racialisation in South Africa. *African Identities* 18(4): 363–376

Thurman H (1966) Desegregation, integration, and the beloved community. https://www.bu.edu/htpp/files/2017/06/Desegregation-Integration-and-the-Beloved-Community.Sept_1966.pdf

Vahed G (2006) Muslims in post-apartheid South Africa. A model of integration? http://www.onislam.net/english/politics/africa/431271.html.

Vawda S (2017) Migration and Muslim Identities: Malawians and Senegalese Muslims in Durban, South Africa. *Journal for the Study of Religion* 30(2): 32–74

Wadud A (2002) 'A'ishah's Legacy'. *New Internationalist Magazine* 345(1). http://newint.org/features/2002/05/01/aishahs-legacy/

Wadud A (2006) *Inside the Gender Jihad: Women's reform in Islam*. Oneworld

Walker M (2005) Rainbow nation or new racism? Theorizing race and identity formation in South African higher education. *Race Ethnicity and Education* 8(2): 129–146

Wing AK & Smith MN (2006) Critical race feminism lifts the veil? Muslim women, France, and the headscarf ban. *UC Davis Law Review* 39(3): 743–790

Wing AK (ed.) (2003) *Critical Race Feminism: A reader* (2nd edn). New York University Press

Woolman S & Fleisch B (2006) South Africa's unintended experiment in school choice: How the National Education Policy Act, the South Africa Schools Act and the Employment of Educators Act create the enabling conditions for quasi-markets in schools. *Education and the Law* 18(1): 31–75

Yancy G (2005) Whiteness and the return of the black body. *The Journal of Speculative Philosophy* 19(4): 215–241

Yancy G (2008) *Black Bodies, White Gazes: The continuing significance of race*. Rowman & Littlefield

Yancy G (2012) *Look, a White! Philosophical essays on whiteness*. Temple University Press

Yancy G & Butler J (2015) What's wrong with 'All Lives Matter'? https://eafework.expressions.syr.edu/wp-content/uploads/2017/02/Whats-Wrong-With-All-Lives-Matter.pdf

Young R (2003) *Postcolonialism: A very short introduction*. Oxford University Press

Young R (2009) What is the postcolonial? *Ariel* 40 (1): 13–25

Index

9/11 96, 98–99

A
academe, women in 93
ACSA *see* Airports Company South Africa
activism 20, 132–133
Adhikari, M 79–81
administrative staff at schools 56, 65
agency 104–105, 107, 109–110, 120
Ahmed, L 106
Ahmed, Sara 16–17, 41, 53, 68, 91, 104, 108–109
airports 99–102
Airports Company South Africa (ACSA) 100–102
Alcalde, MA 93
'All Lives Matter' 88
Al-Qaradawi, Y 106
alumni 56, 57–58, 71
Alvesson, M 22
Anderson, L 22
androcentrism 18
Anglo-normative epistemologies 6–7
anti-apartheid activism 11–12, 82, 119–120
anti-feminist movement 121–122
apartheid
   anti-apartheid activism 11–12, 82, 119–120
   forced removals 2–3, 15–16, 38, 43, 70
   legacy of 11, 40, 42, 52–53, 74–75, 90–91
   objective of 77
   oppression under 2–3, 89
   racial categorisation under 80, 116–117, 125–127
   racism and 32
   schools and 36, 48, 126

Appiah, KA 31
Arabs 104
art vs science 20–21
assimilation 50, 105, 107
attachment and detachment 124–125
autoethnographies 9–10, 18–23

B
Badran, M 28, 129
Bantu Education Act 48–49
'Bantu', use of term 77–78
Barlas, A 128
Barthes, R 4–5
belonging 89, 120–125
Benhabib, S 127–128
Bernal, DD 8
Bhabha, HK 10
binary constructions 7–9
'Black Lives Matter' 88
'black', use of term 78
bodies
   hermeneutics of the body 64
   Muslim female 127–128
   objectification of 103
   terrorism and 104
Butler, Judith 51–52, 88, 128–129

C
CCMA *see* Commission for Conciliation, Mediation and Arbitration
child-rearing 24–25
Christianity 103, 121–122, 123, 126

Christian National Education (CNE) 49, 51, 126
cleaning staff (support staff) at schools 56, 65
CNE *see* Christian National Education
colonialism 7, 10, 24–25, 27, 32, 52–53, 64–65, 74–75
'coloureds' 28–29, 32–33, 43, 78–83, 86, 94, 117, 125
'coming in' 24–25
Commission for Conciliation, Mediation and Arbitration (CCMA) 69–70, 71
communities 111–112, 124–127
competence and incompetence 4, 39, 70, 86–87
   see also standards
constellations of oppression 75
Constitution of South Africa 126–127
contexts 38
Cooke, M 95–96
cosmopolitanism 96
Coste, F 121–122
counter-narrative, autoethnography as 18–23
COVID-19 pandemic 3, 100
'critical fabulation' 8
critical race feminism 11, 29–30
critical reflection 23
criticism 13–14, 118–119
cultural milieu 95, 122
curricula 40–41, 49–51

INDEX

D
DA *see* Democratic Alliance
Das, V 3, 5–6, 38
Davids, Nuraan
   as academic 11–12, 83–86, 94, 103
   on airports 99–102
   childhood of 1–3, 15–16
   doctoral study 112
   father of 14–15, 16, 47
   mother of 85
   security guard incident 97–99
   on SGB as parent 56–57, 60
   as teacher 11–12, 32–41, 44–48, 50
deans at universities 93
decolonisation 7
dehumanisation 2–3, 38
Delamont, S 22
Delgado, Richard 29
Democratic Alliance (DA) 81–82
'democratic' norms 104–105
Democratic Party (DP) 81–82
Department of Higher Education and Training (DHET) 90
desegregation 39, 44–52
detachment and attachment 124–125
DHET *see* Department of Higher Education and Training
discursive colonisation 27
disfigurement 4
District 6 70
diversity 55, 87, 89–94, 131–133
domination 75, 132

DP *see* Democratic Party
drug smuggling 101

E
education *see* schools
Egypt 106
elections, April 1994 127
Ellis, C 9, 19, 22
emotion 9, 14–15
employment 43, 70
equality 6, 89–94
Equality Act 45
Erasmus, Z 77–78
erasure 25
essentialism 31, 131–132
exclusion 34, 44, 46, 59, 120–125
experiences 5–6, 12–18, 52–54

F
faith communities 124–127
   see also communities
Farber, D 9
fathers 122–123, 128
fees *see* schools, fees
feminism 11, 18, 23–29, 108–110, 121–122, 128–130
financial capacity 43, 46
'first world' 26–27
flag, South African 34, 44–48
Fleisch, B 58
forced removals 2, 15–16, 38, 43, 70
France 128
'from below' 13–14, 23–30
'from the bottom' 9–11

-151-

funding *see* state funding for schools

G
Geertz, C 19
gender and religion 96, 111–112
gendered spaces, mosques as 113
gendered subaltern 27
gender imparity 93, 129
gender oppression 11, 29, 108
gender pre-judgements 4
gender, universalism of 128–129
generalisability 22
glass ceiling 93–94
Group Areas Act 16, 38, 42–43, 70, 119, 125

H
hajj 113
Hammett, D 80, 81
Hanafi 116, 117
Hanbali 117
Haraway, D 13–14, 21, 133
Hargreaves, J 105
Hartman, Saidiya 5, 8–9
headscarf *see* hijabs
hermeneutics of the body 64
hijabs 4, 86, 92, 98–110, 128
Hoel, N 129
hooks, b 112–113
'How Muslims betray Islam by not allowing women in the mosques' 114–119
human experiences *see* experiences
human resource practices 91
humiliation 98–99
Hussain, F 106

I
identity 28–29, 51, 81, 87, 106, 122
identity politics 20, 83
image-creation of universities 86–87, 91
incompetence and competence 4, 39, 70, 86–87
  see also standards
'Indians' 116–117, 122, 125
individualism 22–23, 133
Indonesia 106
inequality 131–133
Information Scandal 35
infrastructure 43–44
insider-outsider status 84–85, 94
insider perspective 22–23
insulation and retreat 127
integration 44, 51–52
'intentional invisibility' 92
internalised oppression 64–65, 75
intersectionality 96–98
invisibility 92
Islam 99, 116–120, 122, 125–130
Islamic feminism 28, 129–130
Islamic Unity Convention 127
Islamophobia 11–12

J
Jamiatul ulamas of Transvaal and

Natal 119
Jansen, JD 53
Jardim, G 119
Jones, C 94
Jones, Holman 20–21

K
Kaperjol (Afrikaans textbook) 40–41
Kirmani, N 28, 105
knowledge production 6–7, 17–18, 21, 132

L
language, subtleties of 132
learner demographics 42, 46, 47, 56, 65
learner migration 42–44, 46–47, 57
learners 36–37, 41–42, 50, 53–54, 71
learner-to-teacher ratio 60
Lenz, L 121
liberal democracies 104–110
liberalism 22–23, 91
liminality 86, 94
lived experiences *see* experiences
longing 5
Lugones, M 88
Lugones, MC 9, 18, 24, 25, 28

M
madrassahs 112, 115, 125–126
'Malays' 116–117, 122
Maldonado-Torres, N 7

Maliki 117
Mancini, S 107
Mandela, Nelson 50
marginalisation 27, 81, 92
Matsuda, MJ 28
media coverage 70
Mernissi, F 106
migration
    learner 42–44, 46–47, 57
    residential 43–44, 46
minister of education, Western Cape provincial 71–72
minority groups 93–94
Mirza, HS 92, 98
Mirza, Q 129–130
mixed racial ancestry 32, 79
MJC *see* Muslim Judicial Council
Mohanty, C 23–24, 25–26, 108
Mojapelo, Phineas 45
Moslem Mission schools 126
mosques 113–119, 125–126, 128
Mulder, Cornelius Petrus (Connie) 35
'multiple consciousness' 28
Murad, AH 107
Muslim academics 103
Muslim communities 111–112, 126–127
Muslim feminists 28, 129–130
Muslim Judicial Council (MJC) 116, 119
'Muslimwoman' 96–97
Muslim women 11–12, 23, 28, 92, 95–110, 112–120, 123–124, 127–129

Muslim Youth Movement (MYM) 119, 120
myths we have of each other 74

N
national anthem 34
National Party 77–78, 82
'native', use of term 78
New National Party (NNP) 82
9/11 96, 98–99
Nobanda, Nolubabalo 101
no-fee schools 58
nonracialism 80

O
OBE *see* outcomes-based education
objective vs subjective 22
oppression 9, 32, 38, 64–65, 75, 108–110, 128–129
OR Tambo airport 100–102
Orwell, George 3–4, 18–19
Ossewa-Brandwag 35
'othering'
    activism against 20
    humiliation and 97–103
    intersectional 98
    patriarchy and 120–122
    prevalence of 10–12, 131–132
    race and 94
    religion and 12, 97, 105, 111–112
    in schools 50
    in universities 86
    Western culture and 24–26
outcomes-based education (OBE) 40–41, 49, 51
out-of-placeness 34, 87
outrage 72–73

P
pandemic *see* COVID-19 pandemic
paradox, Muslim women as 104–107
parents 59–62, 67–70, 74
Parents for Change (PfC) 55–56, 60–67, 69–73
patriarchy 11, 106–108, 111–113, 120–130
PfC *see* Parents for Change
Pillay, D 19–20
Poerwandari, EK 23
policies 49–53, 59, 90–92
'Policy Framework for Education and Training, A' 49
Population Registration Act 77–78
postcolonialism 5–12, 23–30, 52–54, 81, 129, 131–133
power relations 49, 75, 98–99, 108, 132
principals (schools) 34, 41, 45–46, 50, 56, 59, 61–62, 66–69, 72
private–public division 129
private schools 43
public–private division 129
public transport 46–47

Q
quintile system 58–59

Qur'an 95, 115, 117, 122–123, 125, 129

R
race as a 'social kind' 31–32
raced and raced-gendered epistemologies 8
racial categorisation 31, 77–80, 82
racial discrimination 4, 28–29, 32, 45
racial identities 81
racial privileging 80, 88–89
racism 31–32, 40–41, 47, 50, 61–62, 91
recognition 41, 87, 94
recruitment at universities 86–87
redress 87–88
reliability 22
religion
    gender and 96, 111–112
    patriarchy and 129–130
    pre-judgements and 4
representations 110, 112
research 19–21
restorative return to homes 43
restorative, stories as 8–9
retreat and insulation 127

S
salaries of teachers 56
Santos, BD 74–75, 131, 132
Schlafly, P 123
School Governing Bodies (SGBs) 55–62, 66–69, 71–72, 74
School Management Team (SMT) 59, 66, 68, 73
schools
    Christian National Education (CNE) 49, 51, 126
    curricula 40–41, 49–51
    desegregation of 39, 44–52
    education departments 48, 51
    fees 44, 46, 56, 58–59, 60
    functionality of 55
    management in 56, 59
    for Muslim children 127
    no-fee 58
    as political tools 73–74
    quintile system 58–59
    'school choice' 57–58
    state funding for 48, 58–59
    textbooks 40–41
    see also teachers
science vs art 20–21
Scott, JW 17–18
September 11 attacks 96, 98–99
service delivery 43–44
SGBs *see* School Governing Bodies
Shafi'i 116–117
Sherry, S 9
Shia 116–118
Shofia, N 106
silence 9, 23, 132
slave trade 8
SMT *see* School Management Team
smuggling of cocaine 101
social media 71

South African Human Rights Commission 102
South African Schools Act 55, 58, 59
Sparkes, AC 5
Spelman, EV 9, 18, 24, 25, 28
Spivak, GC 27, 89
standards 39, 47, 57, 62, 68
  see also competence and incompetence
state funding for schools 48, 58–59
state power 127–128
Stellenbosch University 90–91
stereotypes 104
St. Mark's Anglican church 70
storytelling 6, 8–11, 18–19, 53–54
students 103
subjectivity 16, 22
subjugated status 26–27
Subramaniam, M 93
Sunnah 95, 117
Sunni 116–118
support staff (cleaning staff) at schools 56, 65

T
teacher (Anele) 66–72
teachers
  appointments of 59–60
  demographics 47, 53, 56, 65, 73–74
  at Erica High 44–48, 50
  minority group 53
  policy reform and 50–54
  re-employment of retired 56
  salaries of 56, 60
terrorism 96, 98–99, 104–105
textbooks 40–41
'thick descriptions' 19
thickness of patriarchy 124
'third world' feminist theory 25–27
'third world' women 26–27, 108
Thurman, Howard 49, 51, 52
transformation 55, 72–73, 78–79, 86–87, 90–91
transformative writing 30
transition to democracy, South African 36–39, 42–43, 52
transport, public 46–47
truth 16–17

U
ulama 115–116, 119–120
United States (US) 121–122
Universities South Africa (USAf) 93
University of the Western Cape (UWC) 33
US *see* United States
USAf *see* Universities South Africa
UWC *see* University of the Western Cape

V
validity 22
values 105
Vawda, S 127

veil *see* hijabs
Verwoerd, Hendrik 48–49
vice-chancellors at universities 93
violence 38
visibility 92
Vorster, BJ 34–35
vulnerabilities 21

W
Wadud, A 123
'War on Terror' 104–105
Warsaw Chopin airport 99–100
WCED *see* Western Cape Education Department
Western Cape 81, 114
Western Cape Education Department (WCED) 65–66, 71–72
Western culture and values 7, 11, 79, 108
Western feminism 23–28, 108–110
Western 'War on Terror' narrative 104
Western whiteness 27
'white'/'black' dichotomy 87–88
whiteness 27, 51–53, 68, 73
'white' supremacy 48, 77, 82, 126
'Why I write' 3–4

Wing, AK 29
witnessing 125
women
  in academe 93
  experiences of 11
  glass ceiling 93–94
  minority groups 93
  Muslim 11–12, 23, 28, 92, 95–110, 112–120, 123–124, 127–129
  patriarchy and 120–122
  storytelling 18
  'third world' women 26–27, 108
  in United States 121
  voice of 28
'women in mosques' campaign 114
'Women of Waqf' 114
'Women's Rights Campaign' 120
Woolman, S 58
writers, motives of 3–4

Y
Yancy, G 31–32, 64
Young, R 6–8, 52

Z
Zille, Helen 72

About the author

Nuraan Davids is a Professor of Philosophy of Education in the Department of Education Policy Studies, Faculty of Education at Stellenbosch University, South Africa. Her primary research interests include democratic citizenship education, Islamic philosophy of education, and philosophy of higher education. She is a co-editor of the Routledge series, *World Issues in the Philosophy and Theory of Higher Education*; co-editor-in-chief of the *Journal of Education in Muslim Societies*; associate editor of the *South African Journal of Higher Education*; editorial board member of *Ethics and Education*. Recent books (with Y Waghid) include: *Democratic Education as Inclusion* (Rowman & Littlefield – Lexington Series, 2022); *Academic Activism in Higher Education: A living philosophy for social justice* (Springer, 2021); *Teaching, Friendship & Humanity* (Springer, 2020); *Teachers Matter: Educational philosophy and authentic learning* (Rowman & Littlefield – Lexington Series, 2020).